Better Homes and Gardens®

ENCYCLOPEDIA
of
COOKING

Volume 18

Tempt appetites with the wonderful aroma of homemade bread baked in the oven. This version, Three-Flour Bread, is prepared with all-purpose, whole wheat, and rye flours.

On the cover: For a truly elegant dinner, feature Standing Rib Roast surrounded by crisp and puffy Individual Yorkshire Puddings, which are baked separately in custard cups.

BETTER HOMES AND GARDENS BOOKS
NEW YORK • DES MOINES
Meredith Corporation, 1971. All Rights Reserved.
Printed in the United States of America.
First Printing.
Library of Congress Catalog Card Number: 73-129265
SBN 696-02018-1

WHEAT—The grain of a widely produced cereal grass. Wheat has been so basic to man's diet that it is called the "staff of life," and the term "daily bread" (made from wheat) symbolizes life's necessities.

Wheat shares honors only with rice as the leading food for the world's population. In the United States, Europe, and western Asia wheat is the predominant cereal grain. Only in the Orient and in Africa is rice more prominent.

Exactly where wheat originated is uncertain because wheat does not preserve well for archaeological purposes. Wheat is thought to be from the area considered the birthplace of mankind, southwestern Asia. It was used for food thousands of years ago, and there are records that reveal that the Chinese honored cereals in ceremonies as early as 2800 B.C.

Ancient tribes probably came across wheat in their wanderings. Finding the seeds good to eat, they returned to the wheat fields year after year. In time, they found that the grain could be stored and used both as food during the winter and as seed in the spring. As man began to fashion shelter so that he could stay near his crops, the land best suited to crop growth attracted settlers, who joined together in communities for mutual protection. In this way, wheat cultivation contributed greatly to civilization.

Neolithic man developed tools for wheat cultivation. He used a pointed stick for a plow and a crude sickle for harvesting. Even today, in some of the less developed areas of the world, similar tools are used for harvesting the crops.

Primitive man saw the relationship of wheat to life and incorporated wheat into his religion. The Egyptians believed that the goddess, Isis, discovered wheat in the country now called Lebanon.

The ancient Greeks worshiped Demeter, the grain goddess. The corresponding figure among Roman deities was Ceres, whose name evolved into "cereal." Unlike other gods, who, according to legend, could be arbitrary and cruel, Demeter was a provident, kind figure. She was worshiped not in the bloody sacrifices that were made to other gods, but in humble acts—petitions for a bountiful harvest.

Wheat has played a major role in shaping world history. "The first word in war is spoken by guns, but the last word has always been spoken by bread," said former President Herbert Hoover, who served as Chief of the American Relief Administration after World War I. History offers numerous examples to support his statement. For example, Napoleon's armies advanced so rapidly into Russia that food supplies were left far behind. The Russians destroyed food as they retreated, so when the tide of war turned, the French could not get any food.

Wheat is not native to North America. The Spaniards introduced wheat to Mexico in the 1500s, and British colonists brought wheat to America in 1607.

The development of wheat as a crop is an important chapter in the history of the American colonies. During the early years of colonial America, New Jersey, Pennsylvania, and Maryland were called the "bread colonies" because the people there were able to produce wheat beyond their own needs and export to their neighbors.

As the frontier moved west, so did the center of wheat production. Wheat was a good crop for pioneers. It requires less manpower per acre produced than most other grains, and it has comparatively good keeping qualities. Also, the frontier provided the wide stretches of land needed for wheat cultivation. These factors and the immense popularity of wheat foods made wheat a leading crop.

The outcome of the American Civil War has been described as a victory of bread over cotton. In the North enough wheat was grown to feed the Union army and the civilians. The South's principal product, cotton, could not be eaten.

Wheat classifications: There are many varieties of wheat, each named according to the morphology of the grain, plus the area where it is grown and its intended use. Wheat belongs to the genus *Triticum*, which includes several species, among them being common or bread wheat. Wheat varieties are divided into "hard" and "soft" varieties. Hard wheat contains a stronger quality gluten (elastic protein substance) than do the soft wheat varieties. The varieties can be further divided into winter and spring wheats, based on planting times. In mild climates, such as that found in the Middle Great Plains, wheat is planted in the fall. It is called "winter wheat" and reaches maturity in June and July. In the states farther north, wheat is planted after the threat of frost is past and is called "spring wheat."

The major classes of wheat are hard red spring, hard red winter, durum, soft red winter, white, and red durum. The hard spring and winter wheats are used for bread flour; durum wheat, for pasta products; and soft red winter and white wheat, for pastry flour. Red durum is used for livestock feed.

In the United States, Kansas has been the leading producer of wheat in most of the years of the twentieth century. North Dakota has been on occasion a leading producer, but normally Kansas grows between one-sixth to one-fourth of the nation's total wheat crop.

How wheat is grown: In appearance the plant is slender and golden-colored, and is usually two to four feet high, but it can reach seven feet high. The kernels of the wheat plant are produced in spikes at the head of the stem. The head has four to ten rows of two to over ten kernels.

The wheat kernel is made up of three parts: endosperm, bran, and germ. The endosperm is the starchy interior which makes up about 83 percent of the kernel. Most of the protein in wheat is in the endosperm. The bran is the outer coat, which accounts for 14½ percent of the kernel. The bran is rich in the B vitamins, especially niacin. The germ is the embryo or sprouting section, making up 2½ percent of the kernel. It is usually separated from the rest of the kernel because its fat content limits the keeping qualities. The germ is especially high in thiamine.

How wheat is harvested and processed: Today's child may be confused by references to haystacks, such as the one that cradled "Little Boy Blue." Although once familiar on the rural landscape, they left when modern farm machinery arrived.

In 1831 Cyrus McCormick first demonstrated his mechanical reaper. Since that time, farm machinery has reduced the time required to harvest wheat.

After harvest, grain is stored by the farmer for later sale or is shipped to elevators. At the elevator, a sample of grain is taken from each load and a price is set according to the grade, weight, protein content, and moisture content. Market conditions also affect price. From the country elevator, wheat is shipped to larger storage facilities, either at mills or in silolike bins of a terminal elevator.

At the mill, wheat is made into flour. There are four steps to milling flour: cleaning, tempering, grinding, and post treating. During cleaning, the grain is separated from foreign material and each kernel is scoured clean. Tempering involves adding moisture, which helps separate the outer coatings of bran from the endosperm. During the grinding step, the wheat flows through metal corrugated rollers to give what millers call "the first break." The bran is removed and particles are sized and graded. The grinding continues until the endosperm is freed as much as possible from the bran and germ. The post treatment, depending on the future use of the flour may include blending, maturing, enriching, bleaching.

Delicately spiced nut bread

Sandwich slices of Whole Wheat Nut Bread → together with cream cheese, then cut in triangles, or serve thin slices with butter.

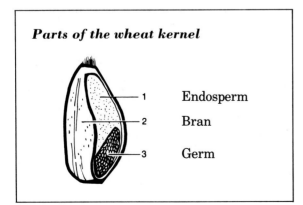

Parts of the wheat kernel

1 Endosperm

2 Bran

3 Germ

Nutritional value: The major wheat food in the United States is baked bread. About 98 percent of the products from commercial bakers are made of white flour, which is made from the endosperm (the natural nutrients of the bran and germ have been removed). The endosperm contains protein, the B vitamins, and carbohydrate.

To compensate for this lack of nutrients, enrichment of the bread is now required in many of the states and in Puerto Rico. In actual practice, all family flours are enriched as is much of the commercially baked standard white bread.

Enrichment first came about as a result of surveys taken during the 1930s, which showed that poor diets were widespread. During the Second World War, concern for improving nutrition grew. The **National Nutrition Conference for Defense** in 1941 set up standards for the enrichment of bread and flour with thiamine, riboflavin, niacin, and iron. Flour products were chosen for enrichment because the members of the conference felt that these products were the ones in most use.

Wheat is also used for breakfast cereals, of which the nutritional value varies with the processing. Look on the package label for specific nutrition information.

Products from wheat: Wheat that is milled into flour is used at home in two ways: as flour and as commercially baked products. Packaged flour includes both all-purpose and cake flour, which are available in most supermarkets. Whole wheat flour is also available, but it is not as widely used as the all-purpose type.

Gluten, a protein in flour, gives baked goods structure. The gluten in all-purpose flour is stronger and more elastic than that in cake flour, making all-purpose flour suitable for breads. The gluten that is present in cake flour produces baked products that are tender.

Flour is also used in prepared mixes for cakes, breads, rolls, cookies, and pancakes. These packaged products account for a high percentage of the flour that is milled and used in the home. The forerunner of mixes is self-rising flour, which millers created by adding a leavening agent and salt to flour.

In addition to its use in baked products, flour is also used as a thickener in cooking. For example, soups, sauces, and gravies are often thickened with flour.

Because of flour's many uses, most homemakers have all-purpose flour on hand at all times. Some homemakers also keep cake flour for use in delicately structured cakes. However, flour does not keep well indefinitely. Use it within a year of purchase. A covered container or canister in a cool place is best for storage.

Most of the flour produced in the United States is used by the commercial bakers. It reaches the table in the form of breads, rolls, cookies, crackers, cakes, and pastries. Snack foods made from flour are also becoming very popular.

Wheat also appears in cereal boxes in a wide array of forms: puffed wheat, wheat flakes, bran flakes, and shredded wheat are just a few. These cereals are ready to eat without further cooking.

Other wheat cereals need to be cooked before eating. Those served hot include wheat meal, malted breakfast food, and farina. Rolled wheat is also available either as a breakfast food or as an ingredient in baked products. Breakfast foods can be shelf-stored, but they should be used within three months of purchase.

Other wheat products that are available in addition to flour, mixes, commercially baked products, and cereals include bulgur, pasta products, and wheat germ.

Bulgur is one of the oldest forms of wheat. It is enjoying renewed popularity and is usually served as a meat accompaniment. Its taste is similar to that of wild rice. Bulgur is wheat that has been parboiled, dried, and partially debranned.

The pasta products include macaroni, spaghetti, noodles, and the many variations of each. Pasta foods made from durum wheat are excellent in color, flavor, and in holding shape when cooked.

Wheat germ is the germ section of the kernel, which has been separated from the endosperm and bran in milling. Processed wheat germ can be added to breakfast cereals or used in baked goods for added flavor and nutrition. (See *Cereal, Durum Wheat, Flour, Grain, Macaroni* for additional information.)

Wheat Bread

Flavored with shredded wheat cereal—

> 2 packages active dry yeast
> 4¾ to 5 cups sifted all-purpose
>   flour
> 2¼ cups milk
> ⅓ cup honey
> ¼ cup butter or margarine
> 1 teaspoon salt
>   • • •
> 1½ cups crushed shredded wheat
>   cereal (3 large biscuits)

In large mixer bowl combine yeast and *2 cups* of the flour. Heat the milk, honey, butter, and salt just till warm, stirring occasionally to melt butter. Stir the wheat cereal into milk; add to dry mixture in mixing bowl. Beat at low speed with electric mixer for ½ minute, scraping sides of bowl constantly. Beat 3 minutes at high speed. By hand, stir in enough of remaining flour to make a moderately stiff dough. Turn out on lightly floured surface; knead till smooth and satiny, 5 to 8 minutes.

Shape into ball; place in greased bowl, turning once to grease surface. Cover; let rise in warm place till double, about 1 hour. Punch down. Cut into 2 portions. Shape in smooth ball; cover and let rest 10 minutes. Shape into 2 loaves. Place in 2 greased 8½x4½x2⅝-inch loaf pans. Cover and let rise till double, 30 to 45 minutes. Bake at 375° till done, about 40 to 45 minutes. Cover loosely with foil during the last 20 minutes if the loaves brown too quickly. Makes 2 loaves.

Curried Wheat Snacks

> 6 tablespoons butter or margarine
> ½ to 1 teaspoon curry powder
> ¼ teaspoon onion salt
> ⅛ teaspoon gound ginger
> 3 cups spoon-sized shredded wheat
>   biscuits

Melt butter in large skillet. Blend in seasonings. Add shredded wheat and toss to coat with butter. Heat about 5 minutes over low heat, stirring frequently. Drain on paper toweling. Serve warm. (Or reheat in oven just before serving.) Makes 3 cups.

Three-Flour Bread

Pictured on page 2450—

> 2 packages active dry yeast
> 1½ cups whole wheat flour
> ½ cup rye flour
> 3¼ to 3½ cups sifted all-purpose
>   flour
> 2 cups milk
> ½ cup brown sugar
> 3 tablespoons shortening
> 2 tablespoons granulated sugar
> 1 tablespoon salt

Combine yeast, whole wheat flour, rye flour, and *1 cup* of the all-purpose flour in a large mixer bowl. Heat together milk, brown sugar, shortening, granulated sugar, and salt just till warm. Add to dry mixture. Beat at low speed of electric mixer for ½ minute, scraping bowl constantly. Beat 3 minutes at high speed. Stir in enough of the remaining all-purpose flour to make a moderately stiff dough. Turn out onto floured surface; knead 8 to 10 minutes.

Place in greased bowl, turning once. Cover; let rise till double, 1½ hours. Punch down; let rest 10 minutes. Shape into 2 loaves; place in 2 greased 8½x4½x2½-inch loaf dishes. Let rise till double, 45 to 60 minutes. Bake at 375° till done, about 40 minutes. Makes 2.

Quickly turn ready-to-eat breakfast cereal into Curried Wheat Snacks, a sophisticated tidbit that is served while it is still warm.

Whole Wheat Nut Bread

A spicy quick bread—

       1 cup sifted all-purpose flour
       2 teaspoons baking powder
     1/2 teaspoon ground cinnamon
     1/4 teaspoon salt
     1/4 teaspoon ground nutmeg
     1/4 teaspoon ground allspice
     1/2 cup whole wheat flour
              • • •
     1/4 cup butter or margarine
     3/4 cup sugar
       2 eggs
     2/3 cup milk
     1/2 teaspoon vanilla
     1/2 cup chopped walnuts

Sift together the all-purpose flour, baking powder, cinnamon, salt, nutmeg, and allspice. Stir in the whole wheat flour.

Cream together the butter or margarine and sugar. Add eggs, one at a time, beating well after each addition. Add dry ingredients to creamed mixture alternately with milk and vanilla. Beat smooth after each addition. Stir in the chopped walnuts. Turn into a greased 8½x4½x2⅝-inch loaf pan. Bake at 350° till loaf tests done, 50 to 55 minutes. Cool 10 minutes. Remove from pan. Makes 1 loaf.

WHEY *(hwā, wā)*—The thin, watery liquid part of milk that is left after the curds have formed, as when milk is curdled for making cheese. Whey, as well as the curd, is used in making some kinds of cheeses.

WHIP—1. To beat air into a food, such as egg whites or cream, lightening its texture and increasing its volume. **2.** An alternate name for a whisk, which is often used in the whipping process. **3.** A light dessert that is made fluffy and delicate by adding beaten cream or egg whites or by beating a gelatin mixture before it is completely set. The dessert is frequently flavored with fruit pulp, such as prunes or plums, or with other ingredients, such as chocolate and/or nuts. Whips are light desserts, making them a perfect ending for a hearty meal. (See *Dessert, Whisk* for additional information.)

Chocolate-Pecan Whip

       1 envelope unflavored gelatin
           (1 tablespoon)
     1/4 cup sugar
           Dash salt
       2 egg yolks
     1½ cups milk
       1 teaspoon vanilla
       2 egg whites
     1/4 cup sugar
       1 cup whipping cream
     1/2 cup semisweet chocolate pieces
     1/4 cup broken pecans

In saucepan thoroughly mix gelatin, 1/4 cup sugar, and salt. Beat together egg yolks and milk; stir into gelatin mixture. Cook and stir over low heat till slightly thickened. Add vanilla; chill till partially set.

Beat egg whites till soft peaks form. Gradually add 1/4 cup sugar, beating till stiff peaks form; fold into gelatin mixture.

Whip the cream. Reserve *half* of the whipped cream and a few chocolate pieces for garnish; set aside. Chop remaining chocolate pieces. Fold remaining whipped cream, chopped chocolate, and the nuts into gelatin mixture. Spoon into dessert dishes; chill. Garnish with reserved chocolate and whipped cream, and additional pecans, if desired. Makes 6 to 8 servings.

Chilled Prune Whip

     1½ cups whole prunes
     1½ cups water
       3 egg whites
     1/4 teaspoon salt
     1/3 cup sugar
       2 tablespoons lemon juice
     1/4 cup chopped pecans

In saucepan combine prunes and water; bring to boiling. Cover and simmer 10 minutes; allow to cool in liquid. Drain. With kitchen shears, snip prunes from pits in small pieces; set aside. In large mixer bowl beat egg whites with salt till soft peaks form. Gradually add sugar, beating till stiff peaks form. In small mixer bowl combine prunes and lemon juice; beat till well blended. Fold into egg whites; fold in nuts. Spoon the mixture into dessert dishes; chill. Makes 6 to 8 servings.

Plum Whip

  1 envelope unflavored gelatin
     (1 tablespoon)
¼ cup cold water
  1 7¾-ounce jar strained plums
     (junior food)
10 drops red food coloring
  1 tablespoon lemon juice
¾ cup milk
  2 egg whites
  3 tablespoons sugar
½ cup frozen whipped dessert
     topping, thawed

Soften gelatin in cold water. Heat strained plums in a saucepan till boiling. Add softened gelatin, food coloring, and lemon juice. Stir till gelatin dissolves. Add milk. Cool till partially thickened. Beat egg whites till soft peaks form; gradually add sugar and beat till stiff peaks form. Add plum mixture gradually and beat till fluffy. Fold in the thawed dessert topping. Spoon into sherbet glasses. Chill thoroughly. Before serving, top with additional thawed whipped dessert topping, if desired. Makes 6 to 8 servings.

WHIPPED TOPPING – A fluffy nondairy product used to garnish desserts. Some toppings are used also as an ingredient in desserts or salads for volume and flavor.

Various forms of whipped toppings are available on the market. One type comes frozen in covered bowls, needing only to be thawed before use. Another topping that comes frozen needs to be thawed and whipped before it is used. Pressurized containers of whipped dessert topping are also available and are ready for use. In addition, you'll find dessert topping mixes on the supermarket shelf. These can be made into whipped toppings by adding liquid and beating, following the directions on the package label.

A light, refreshing dessert

Plum Whip, which gets its delicate color and flavor from a jar of junior food, is sure to be a favorite with the adults, too.

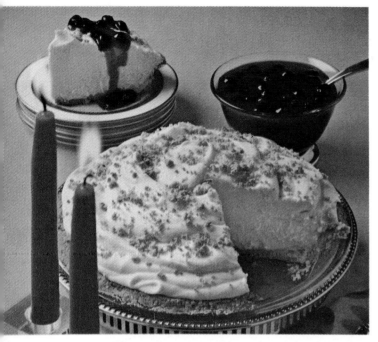

Whipped cream adds richness and a light texture to Lemon Frost Pie. To serve, spoon fresh Blueberry Sauce over wedges of the pie.

WHIPPING CREAM—A milk product containing a minimum of 30 percent milk fat that can be whipped until fluffy, thickened, and doubled in volume. It is also called heavy cream or heavy whipping cream if it has more than the minimum amount of milk fat.

There are specified amounts of milk fat for whipping cream. Light whipping cream must contain 30 to 36 percent, while heavy cream or heavy whipping cream must contain at least 36 percent.

Whipping cream adds calories and a small amount of vitamin A to the diet. One tablespoon of light whipping cream has 45 calories; heavy cream, 52 calories.

The uses of whipping cream are numerous. It's a favorite dessert topper, plain or flavored, and it is also used as an ingredient in chilled and frozen desserts, supplying both volume and richness. Whipped cream and nuts on an ice cream sundae add a special note. Whipping cream is also used in other dishes, such as vegetables. (See also *Cream*.)

Volcano Potatoes

    4 or 5 medium potatoes, peeled
       Milk
½ cup whipping cream
    2 ounces sharp process American
       cheese, shredded (½ cup)

Cook potatoes till tender; drain and mash. Season with salt and pepper. Whip potatoes with enough hot milk (about ¾ cup) to make fluffy. Pile into greased 8-inch round baking dish, mounding into volcano shape. Make a crater in center. Whip cream; fold in cheese. Pour over potatoes. Bake at 350° till lightly browned, about 20 minutes. Serves 6.

Whipping cream know-how

● Whipping cream doubles in volume when whipped; thus, one cup of cream will yield about two cups of whipped cream. Do not overwhip the cream or it may turn to butter.
● Use chilled cream that is at least 24 hours old. If the cream is too warm, it won't whip.
● For best volume, don't try to whip more than two cups of cream at a time.
● A chilled bowl, preferably with sloping sides and deep enough to allow the cream to double, is the best container to use.
● Use chilled beaters of an electric mixer or a chilled rotary beater to rapidly whip the cream until it mounds and holds shape.
● To sweeten whipped cream, add two to four tablespoons of sugar per cup of unwhipped cream after the whipping process is almost completed. If sugar is added too soon, the volume and stiffness of the final product will be decreased. A small amount of vanilla can be added for extra flavor.
● To freeze mounds of whipped cream for a dessert topper, whip cream and add sugar and flavoring, if desired. Drop from spoon into mounds on waxed paper-lined baking sheet. Freeze till mounds are firm. Place in freezer container; seal, label, and freeze. Store in freezer up to three months. When ready to use, place frozen mounds on servings of dessert. Let stand at room temperature about 20 minutes.

Lemon Frost Pie

      1 cup sifted all-purpose flour
    ½ cup butter or margarine
      2 tablespoons sugar
    ¼ teaspoon salt
            •   •   •
      2 egg whites
    ⅔ cup sugar
      2 teaspoons grated lemon peel
    ¼ cup lemon juice
      5 drops yellow food coloring
      1 cup whipping cream
        Blueberry Sauce

Mix flour, butter, 2 tablespoons sugar, and salt till crumbly. Place ⅓ cup crumb mixture in baking dish; press remaining into greased and floured 9-inch pie plate. Bake both at 375° for 12 to 15 minutes; cool. Combine egg whites, ⅔ cup sugar, lemon peel and juice, and food coloring; beat to stiff peaks. Whip cream; fold into lemon mixture. Turn into pie shell; top with crumbs. Chill or freeze.

Serve with *Blueberry Sauce:* Combine ⅔ cup sugar, 1 tablespoon cornstarch, and dash salt. Add ⅔ cup water. Cook and stir till thick; cook 2 minutes more. Add 2 cups fresh blueberries; return to boiling. Chill.

WHISK – **1.** A utensil made of wire loops fastened to a handle, designed for beating foods till frothy or fluffy. Whisks range in size from a tiny one suitable for beating one egg to large balloon-shaped whisks for beating doughs. Whisks are also called whips. **2.** To beat or whip foods, such as cream or eggs, till frothy.

WHISKEY, WHISKY – A spirit distilled from the fermented mash of a grain. According to United States regulations, whiskey must be distilled at less than 190 proof, be diluted to a strength of from 80 to 110 proof, and be aged in charred oak barrels. The word whiskey is a derivation of a Celtic word meaning "water of life." Irish and Americans prefer the first spelling; Scottish and Canadians, the latter.

Both Ireland and Scotland are closely allied to the evolution of whiskey. In fact, both countries still vie for the claim to whiskey's origin. In the United States, too, whiskeymaking was initiated by the colonists of Irish and Scottish descent who first operated pot stills for their personal consumption shortly after the American Revolution.

Growth of whiskey production in the United States was a logical result of America winning its independence. After the Revolution, the import duty placed on molasses made rum, once the most important colonial spirit, unprofitable if not almost impossible to produce. Whiskey stills increased particularly in areas of Maryland, Virginia, and the Carolinas where the grains used for whiskey were readily available to anyone who wanted them and at a reasonable price.

As Irish and Scottish pioneers settled farther west into western Pennsylvania, Kentucky, and Tennessee, they found that whiskey production was even more economically necessary. The equivalent of 24 bushels of grain in the form of whiskey could be transported to eastern markets as opposed to only 4 bushels of actual grain. The distillery, first a family then a community project, gradually became an extremely large commercial venture. In less than twenty years after the first distillery was established near Pittsburgh, Pennsylvania, thousands of other distilleries were in operation.

Whiskey production up to this time was not governmentally regulated. But in 1791, when the value of the dollar plummeted, a tax was imposed on whiskey. The distillers' opposition that followed, now called the Whiskey Rebellion, even required the use of military force. Although the tax was repealed in 1802, a whiskey tax was soon here to stay.

How whiskey is produced: All whiskies are based on the general procedures of fermentation and distillation. Many different kinds of whiskies are made simply by varying the grain used or by adding a unique stage of production.

First, the fermenting mixture called the mash is prepared by mixing the dried, crushed grain with hot water. Next, the yeast is added by either the sour or sweet mash methods. For a sour mash, a portion of a previous fermentation is added to the fresh mash. For a sweet mash, only new yeast-starter is used. Fermentation continues for several days.

When the fermented liquid, now known as "low wine" or "distillers' beer," has reached the proper stage, the mixture is pumped into the stills where distillation occurs. The whiskey is distilled one or more times, depending on the type. After distillation, the alcoholic content is reduced by adding water and the liquid is placed in charred oak barrels to age.

Types of whiskies: There are many kinds of whiskies sold in the United States. Some are labeled (and their production controlled) by the country in which the whiskies are distilled. The other types are designated by the grain content.

Bourbon whiskey is the only spirit that was first made in the United States. Bourbon must contain at least 51 percent corn, be distilled at not more than 160° proof, and be aged in new charred oak barrels. It has a full-bodied, sweet flavor.

Canadian whisky is produced in Canada principally from corn, but it also contains some rye, barley, and wheat. The mash is distilled off at a high proof and is filtered before bottling. A minimum of two years aging is required in either new or used barrels. Canadian whisky has a characteristic light, slightly sweet flavor.

Irish whiskey, the product of Ireland, consists mainly of malted plus sprouted barley. Wheat, oats, and a little rye may also be included. Distillation is carried out at a low proof, often as many as three times. The Irish whiskey available in American markets is usually seven or more years old. The liquor has full, smooth body and malt flavor.

Scotch whisky comes from Scotland and is made from peat-dried, malted barley that has been fermented and distilled then blended with a corn-rye whiskey. The barley whiskey is distilled off at 140 proof; the corn-rye whiskey, at 180 proof. The Scotch whisky sold in the United States has been aged over four years. It is light-bodied and has a smoky flavor.

Straight whiskey is legally defined as being distilled at no higher than 160 proof, aged in new charred oak barrels at least two years, reduced to not less than 80 proof in strength, and containing no additives other than water. A straight whiskey has full flavor, body, and aroma. The dominant grain used in the mash (over 51 percent) determines the name of the whiskey—straight Bourbon whiskey if corn; straight rye whiskey if rye; straight wheat whiskey if wheat; straight malt whiskey if barley malt; and straight rye malt whiskey if rye malt. Straight corn whiskey, however, must be distilled from a mash containing at least 80 percent corn. Tennessee whiskey must be produced in the state of Tennessee from at least 51 percent corn. Blended straight whiskey consists of straight whiskies taken from different distilling periods and from different distilleries.

Blended whiskey is a mixture of whiskey and neutral spirits (a liquor of 190 proof or more). At least 20 percent of a blended whiskey must consist of the grain whiskey. Because of the neutral spirits concentration, blended whiskies are naturally lighter in flavor and body than are straight whiskies. Most whiskey sold in the United States is blended.

How to use: Whiskies are used widely in beverages and find lesser use in cooked foods. Some people insist that whiskey is best when consumed straight. Others prefer it on the rocks or with water. Others prefer soda mixtures and cocktail blends such as sours, Manhattans, mint juleps, old-fashioneds, or highballs. When you prepare a soup or a dessert topping try using a whiskey to accent the flavor. Fruit flavors are also complemented with the addition of small amounts of whiskey. (See also *Wines and Spirits.*)

Whiskey Sour

    ½ jigger fresh lemon or lime juice
    2 jiggers Bourbon, Scotch, or rye
    1 teaspoon confectioners' sugar
    3 or 4 ice cubes

Combine all ingredients. Shake well. Strain into a glass. If desired, trim with a lemon slice and maraschino cherry. Makes 1 drink.

WHITEFISH—A saltwater or freshwater fish related to the salmon and trout. A few are found along California's coast, but the majority are found in the colder waters of North America, Europe, and Asia. Those sold in America come from the Great Lakes, Minnesota, and Canada.

Whitefish have green and silvery coloring, large scales, a small mouth with no teeth, and a forked tail fin. These fish average between two and four pounds.

The whole fish and fillets are sold fresh and frozen. Smoked whitefish and roe are also available. The flesh of the whitefish can be cooked by baking, broiling, frying, boiling, or steaming.

Whitefish's nutritional value consists of protein, minerals, and B vitamins. There are about 155 calories in an uncooked piece measuring 3x3x⅞ inches (about 3½ ounces). A 3½-ounce serving of whitefish when stuffed and baked has 215 calories. (See also *Fish*.)

WHITE PEPPER—A light-colored spice made from the berries of a vine called *Piper nigrum*. White pepper is made from the same berries as black pepper, but it has a more subtle flavor and a pale yellow or gray appearance. The white spice is made from mature berries, whereas black pepper is made from immature ones.

In making white pepper, the berries are soaked in water to loosen the outside skin. The skin is rubbed off and the cores, or white peppercorns, are sun-dried. If the pepper is to be ground, this is the next step in production.

White pepper is widely used in Europe as a seasoning. In the United States it is used most often in recipes such as cream sauces and salad dressings, when the dark specks of black pepper are not wanted. White pepper can be substituted for black pepper. (See also *Pepper*.)

WHITE SAUCE—A basic sauce prepared with butter or margarine, flour, milk, cream, or white stock. The sauce is prepared by melting the butter, then blending in flour and seasonings. Liquid is added and the mixture is stirred till thickened and bubbly.

Prepare white sauce in varying thicknesses, according to your needs. For example, use thin white sauce in soups and creamed vegetables, and medium white sauce in scalloped and creamed dishes. Make thick white sauce for croquettes and soufflés. (See also *Sauce*.)

White Sauce

Thin:
- 1 tablespoon butter or margarine
- 1 tablespoon all-purpose flour
- ¼ teaspoon salt
- 1 cup milk

Medium:
- 2 tablespoons butter or margarine
- 2 tablespoons all-purpose flour
- ¼ teaspoon salt
- 1 cup milk

Thick:
- 3 tablespoons butter or margarine
- ¼ cup all-purpose flour
- ¼ teaspoon salt
- 1 cup milk

In a heavy saucepan melt butter or margarine over low heat. Blend in flour, salt, and dash white pepper. Stir till bubbly. Add milk all at once. Cook quickly, stirring constantly till mixture thickens and bubbles. Makes 1 cup.

How to repair white sauce

If white sauce cooks too long, it may become thick and the butter will separate out. To repair the sauce, stir in a little more milk. Then, cook the mixture quickly, stirring constantly, until the sauce bubbles.

WHITE WINE—An almost white to deep gold, dry or sweet wine that is made either by using white grapes or by fermenting purple grapes without skins and seeds.

White wine production usually is more exacting than that for red wines. Controls maintain the color and flavor balance. White wines are usually aged less and reach maturity sooner than red wines.

The largest class of white wines is dinner or table wines, such as Rhine, chablis, or sauterne, and those named for the grape varieties from which they are principally made, such as Riesling, Pinot Chardonnay, and Sauvignon Blanc.

Serve white dinner wines at about 50° and use to complement light-flavored foods, such as poultry, fish, and shellfish. (See also *Wines and Spirits.*)

WHITING—A lean, saltwater fish of the cod family. Other names include silver hake, kingfish, and frostfish. The whiting lives along the New England and English coasts. It has a long, slender body colored brown or green and silver. Identifying lateral lines run the length of the fish. The size can reach as much as 30 inches in length and five pounds in weight.

Whiting sold on the market weigh one to four pounds and usually measure about 12 inches long. They come dressed, drawn, filleted, or in portions, and may be frozen, fresh, or smoked. Boil, steam, or fry this firm, white, tender fish. If butter or shortening is added, broil or bake the fish. (See also *Fish.*)

WHOLE WHEAT—The entire wheat kernel with only the harsh outer hull removed. Because the whole kernel is used, whole wheat products contain the nutrients of the whole grain, including the B vitamins, protein, and minerals. Since the germ is included, whole wheat, and the flour ground from it, does not have the keeping quality of white flour. Buy whole wheat products in small quantities and use up your supply quickly. Whole wheat is also used in cereals. (See *Cereal, Wheat* for additional information.)

WHORTLEBERRY (*hwûr' tuhl ber' ē, wur'-*)—An edible, dark blue to black berry, similar in size to a black currant, found growing in England, northern Europe, and Asia. The sweet flavor of whortleberries is enjoyed fresh during July and August, or in preserves during the off-season. They taste like huckleberries.

WIENER (*wē' nuhr*)—Another name for a frankfurter. (See also *Frankfurter.*)

WIENER SCHNITZEL (*vē' nuhr shnit' suhl*)—A Viennese main dish prepared with veal cutlets, which are breaded, then sautéed in shortening. The name is derived from the German word *schnitzel*, which means a slice of meat or a cutlet. When a fried egg tops the cooked cutlet, you have *Wiener Schnitzel à la Holstein.* The dish is often served with lemon wedges. (See also *Viennese Cookery.*)

Wiener Schnitzel

1½ pounds veal cutlets, ½ inch thick
¼ cup all-purpose flour
1 teaspoon salt
¼ teaspoon pepper
1 beaten egg
1 tablespoon milk
1 cup fine dry bread crumbs
¼ cup salad oil
Lemon wedges

Cut meat into 4 pieces; pound ¼ to ⅛ inch thick. Cut small slits around edges to prevent curling. Coat meat with flour seasoned with salt and pepper. Combine egg and milk. Dip floured cutlets in egg mixture, then in bread crumbs. Cook the meat in hot oil till tender, 2 to 3 minutes on each side. Serve with lemon wedges. Makes 4 servings.

Wiener Schnitzel à la Holstein: Prepare Wiener Schnitzel. In skillet, fry 4 eggs in butter till whites are set. Add 1 tablespoon water. Cover; cook till eggs are done. Place one cooked egg on each veal cutlet. Sprinkle with snipped parsley, if desired.

WILD GAME—A wild animal or bird that is taken for food. (See also *Game.*)

WILD MARJORAM—An alternate name for the herb, oregano. (See also *Oregano.*)

WILD RICE—The seed of an annual marsh grass. The name "wild rice" is only partly accurate. This rice does grow wild along the shallows of lakes, in streams, and in swampy places, but it is not related to the oriental grain that has been called rice for many centuries.

Wild rice, a native of North America, was once an important food for the American Indians. They introduced it to French explorers, who agreed that it was delectable. The French named it wild oats.

Today, about three million pounds of wild rice are harvested yearly in the United States and Canada, with about 60 percent coming from Minnesota.

Wild rice is self-sowing and reaches a height of four to eight feet. The plant has flat, spreading leaves and bears a large cluster of seeds. The grain of wild rice is slender, round, and two to three times longer than white rice. It is dark brown in color and chewy when cooked. Wild rice is somewhat nutlike in flavor.

The industrial revolution has had very little effect on wild rice production. The grain still is harvested from boats, similar to the way it was done before the Europeans came to the New World.

Harvesting wild rice consists of freeing the seeds from the plant. The stalks are bent over the boat and the heads of the plants are knocked with a club that looks like an oversized drumstick. The ripe rice falls into the boat while the un-ripened grains remain on the head of the plant. For this reason, harvesting is done three to four times to get all the ripened rice. Only about 25 percent of the crop is taken; the remainder falls back into the water for reseeding and food for wildlife. However, there are specific regulations set up regarding harvesting. These include size of boat, size of the club used for knocking off the ripened rice, who can harvest the crop, and harvesting times.

The American Indians dried wild rice, then placed it in a hole in the ground that had been lined with animal skins. In order to loosen the hulls, the Indians stamped on the grains. The rice was then transferred to a blanket and tossed up in the air to separate it from the loosened hulls. Today, most rice is harvested and then sold to processors who use machinery to complete the parching, hulling, winnowing, cleaning, and grading.

Wild rice makes about the same contribution to the diet as do other whole grains. It supplies some carbohydrate, calcium, iron, protein, and the B vitamins.

Wild rice is sold as either plain wild rice or wild rice mixed with long-grain white rice. The price of wild rice is high because only 25 percent of the crop is taken and because 100 pounds of the green rice produces 40 pounds of rice suitable for sale. However, the appeal to gourmet tastes makes it worth the extra cost. Wild rice mixed with white rice costs less and contributes much of the eating enjoyment of the unmixed product.

If wild rice is not to be used immediately, it is best to transfer it to a container with a tight-fitting cover.

Unlike regular white rice, wild rice needs to be rinsed before using. Place the amount to be cooked in a pan of warm water, stir, then drain and remove any particles that float to the top. This should be done twice, followed by a rinsing in a strainer. One cup of uncooked wild rice yields three to four cups cooked rice.

Cooked wild rice is used as an accompaniment for game and poultry. It is often used in a stuffing, cooked with other ingredients and used as a main dish, topped with butter, or served with a sauce.

Wild Rice and Mushrooms

Drain one 3-ounce can broiled, sliced mushrooms, reserving liquid. Mix one 10½-ounce can condensed beef broth, mushroom liquid, and enough water to make 2 cups. Add 2 medium onions, finely chopped; bring to boiling. Add ½ cup rinsed wild rice. Reduce heat; simmer, covered, for 20 minutes. Add 1 cup long-grain rice. Return to boil. Reduce heat; simmer, covered, 20 minutes longer. Add mushrooms and 2 tablespoons butter. Heat. Add 2 tablespoons snipped parsley. Serves 6 to 8.

Wild Rice Stuffing

Cook one 6-ounce package long-grain and wild rice mix according to package directions. Cool the rice. Stir in ½ cup chopped celery; one 5-ounce can water chestnuts, drained and sliced; one 3-ounce can chopped mushrooms, drained; ¼ cup butter, melted; and 1 tablespoon soy sauce. Makes about 4 cups stuffing or enough for 4 Cornish game hens.

WINES AND SPIRITS

*A clear and concise primer to help you choose,
use, and enjoy alcoholic beverages.*

Much mystery surrounds the words wines and spirits. Together they conjure up a picture of liquids in dusty bottles and sparkling glasses. Encompassing these liquids are centuries of traditions regarding production, use, and selection in concert with such words as bouquet, body, and flambé.

But there need be nothing mysterious or earthshaking about wines and spirits if you know a little about them. You will have the delightful experience of knowing that you can break the rules, have fun drinking the beverage you like, and use it to best advantage in foods.

The essence of all wines and spirits is fermentation, the frothy interaction of sugar and yeast. Simply said, this wonder of nature changes sugar to alcohol.

Producing alcohol that is not only potable but that tastes and looks good, however, is more complex than this, for an alcoholic product is influenced by the nature of the food used for fermentation as well as by the way it is fermented. Grapes, for example, include sugar and water plus other constituents such as acids, cellulose, and essential oils. Likewise, fermentation is a combination of reactions that change the substances in the juice. These changes give each alcoholic beverage its color, flavor, and bouquet.

How the liquid is fermented and subsequently handled differentiates wines from spirits. A wine is made by fermenting a fruit, vegetable, or herb juice. When the word wine is used by itself, it is commonly held to mean grape wine. Wines made from other fruits carry the name of the fruit, for example, apple wine and cherry wine. A spirit, on the other hand, is a highly alcoholic liquid that has been distilled from juice containing alcohol.

Only in fairly recent times has it been understood how foods are transformed into wines and spirits, but the making of alcoholic beverages dates back to ancient times. Winemaking is by far the oldest of the two techniques. Although distillation was known by some early civilizations, it took some time before the process was used for making alcoholic spirits.

Wines

Although wine was made in China prior to 2000 B.C., the early winemaking that most influenced the Western world began in the "cradle of civilization," the Middle East. Vineyards abounded in Egypt, Palestine, and Persia. A 30,000 gallon winery was located at Gibeon, near Jerusalem, until the city's destruction in 600 B.C.

The history of winemaking coincides with the development of great civilizations. Both the Greeks and Romans worshiped a god of wine. Following the conquest of Gaul, the Romans pursued grape cultivation and winemaking throughout their empire. By the fifteenth century, Europe had become the foremost wine-producing region in the world.

European settlers brought their knowledge of growing grapes and making wine to the Western Hemisphere. Even though native American grapes were already growing profusely on the new land, the colonists began importing cuttings from

A connoisseur's touch

← Cooking with wines and spirits adds gourmet flavor to Snow-Capped Pâté, Scallopine Burgers, Bourbon Balls, and Orange-Rum Cake.

the European vines. Attempts to grow European vines on the East Coast were unsuccessful, but fruitful results were immediate in Mexico and California.

During the 1800s, United States' wine production became commercial in nature, but its growth was soon interrupted. First, a severe predator of grapevines, Phylloxera, infested and almost destroyed the vineyards. Then, in 1920, the United States government's move to prohibit alcohol greatly curtailed wine production.

Following the repeal of Prohibition, there was a quick revival of wineries that produced quality wines. Today, the demand for good wines continues to increase—so much so, in fact, that the United States has become one of the ten largest wine-producing countries.

How wine is produced: Successful winemaking is more than simply letting grapes ferment naturally. Rather, it is a combination of growing quality grapes and caring for the must (pressed grape juice) daily as it ferments and ages.

Since a wine is only as good as the grapes from which it is made, grape cultivation (viticulture) is a vital step in winemaking. Harvesting the grapes at just the right time is one of the most critical steps. As the grapes mature, they are regularly tested for sugar and acid content. A higher sugar concentration is desired for grapes used in making sweet wines than for those used for dry wines.

The science of winemaking (enology) takes over after the grapes are picked. For a white wine, either white grapes are used or the juice of red grapes is expressed and separated from the skins and seeds. If a rosé (pink) or red wine is desired, the juice, skins, and seeds of red grapes ferment together for a time.

Although grape skins are covered with wild yeasts that can initiate fermentation naturally, most winemakers kill the wild yeasts and add special yeast cultures for better control. If a dry wine is desired (one without residual sugar), fermentation continues to completion. (The maximum alcoholic content this wine can attain is about 14 percent.) If a partially or fully sweet wine is desired,

however, fermentation is halted by either adding brandy, using small amounts of a sterilizing substance, filtering, or other means. Addition of brandy often increases the alcoholic content up to 21 percent.

When fermentation has subsided, the wine is still not at its best. Aging in wood (letting the wine rest) permits the characteristic flavor, body, and bouquet to develop. White wines generally age in less time than do the red ones.

Bottling of the wine follows. In the bottle, the flavor and bouquet continue to develop. Wine is the only beverage that changes once it is bottled.

To produce a sparkling, effervescent wine, a dry wine is subjected to a second fermentation in sealed containers prior to the final bottling. When fermentation is complete, the yeast sediment is removed and the wine is bottled.

Wine vinegar, a by-product of wine, is made by introducing acetic acid bacteria to a dry red, rosé, or white wine for a second fermentation. Sometimes, the wine is additionally flavored with herbs such as tarragon.

Classes of wines: For clarification, wines often are categorized into five classes: appetizer, red dinner, white dinner, dessert, and sparkling. Each class name describes the general character or use of the wines within the class.

Appetizer or aperitif denotes wines that are preferred for before-meal or cocktail consumption. In most cases, the dry wines are preferred over the sweet ones. The most well-known appetizer wines are Sherry and Vermouth, but another group, the natural or flavored wines, is rapidly gaining popularity.

Dinner (table) wines are, quite naturally, those customarily served with the main course of the meal. Red dinner wines such as red Burgundies, Clarets, and red Chiantis are predominately dry and rich in taste and sometimes carry a tartness or astringency. The flavor diversity of white dinner wines encompasses very dry and tart to sweet and full-bodied wines. Some of the popular types of white dinner wines are Chablis, Rhine wines, white Burgundies, drier Sauternes, and white Chiantis. Pink Rosé wines, ranging in flavor from sweet to slightly astringent, also fall under the dinner wine category.

Dessert wines, the sweetest and fullest-flavored wines, are served at the last course of the meal. Well-known types include Ports, Muscatels, Tokays, sweet Sherries, and sweeter Sauternes.

Sparkling wines, because of their versatility, taste equally good before, during, or at the end of a meal. The traditional sparkling wines are Champagne and Sparkling Burgundy. Cold Duck is the newest of the sparkling wines.

European wines: The Europeans were the first to perfect winemaking techniques. The people of France, Germany, Italy, and Portugal made the earliest con-

tributions. The wines that they developed are the ones that winemakers throughout the world try to equal or excel.

French wines – Four principal regions produce the French wines that have given this country its reputation: Bordeaux, Burgundy, Champagne, and Alsace. Red Clarets, always-sweet Sauternes, and white Graves wines are produced in and around Bordeaux. Red, white, and sparkling Burgundy wines are produced in the region of Burgundy. From the Champagne region come the sparkling white wines of the same name. Alsace produces the Rhine wines of France such as Riesling and Traminer.

German wines – The best-known German wines are white, made from Riesling grapes, and come from two sectors, the

Tantalize thirsty friends with these drinks. For wine enthusiasts, try Tomato-Vermouth Cocktail, Rosé Frappé, or Summer Sangria (see *Sangria*). Lime Fizz appeals to liqueur lovers.

Wine Chart				
Class	Wine family	Varietal wines in family	Serving temperature	Best with
Appetizer	Sherry (dry) Vermouth Flavored wines		Cool room temperature (60° to 70°) *or* chilled (45° to 55°)	All appetizer foods—canapés, hors d'oeuvres, soups, dips
Red Dinner Wines	Burgundy (red) Claret (Bordeaux) Chianti (red) Rosé	Pinot Noir, Gamay Cabernet Sauvignon, Zinfandel Grignolino	Cool room temperature (60° to 70°) *except* for Rosé Chilled (45° to 50°)	Hearty foods—all red meats including beef, veal, pork, game; cheese, egg, and pasta dishes
White Dinner Wines	Chablis (White Burgundy) Rhine Sauterne (dry) Chianti (white)	Pinot Chardonnay, Folle Blanche Riesling, Sylvaner, Traminer Semillon, Sauvignon Blanc	Chilled (45° to 50°)	Light foods—poultry, fish and shellfish, veal
Dessert Wines	Port Tokay Muscatel Sauterne (sweet) Sherry (sweet)		Cool room temperature (60° to 70°)	All desserts—fruits, nuts, cakes, dessert cheeses
Sparkling Wines	Champagne Sparkling Burgundy Sparkling Rosé Cold Duck		Chilled (40° to 45°)	All foods and occasions

Rhine and Moselle valleys. Rhine wines (Hock wines) may be dry or sweet, and light-bodied or full-bodied. Moselle wines are dry and lighter than are Rhine wines.

Italian wines — Italy is the home of some delicious wines that have won world acclaim. From the Piedmont region come the greatest Italian wines: heavy, red Barolo and Barbaresco, and somewhat sweet, sparkling Asti spumanti. From Tuscany comes Chianti in its traditional straw-covered flasks.

Spanish wines — In Spain as in Italy, many wines are produced. Dry to sweet Sherry must come from the Jerez region. Montilla is dry, sherrylike wine made outside of the Jerez region. The red, white, and rosé Rioja wines of northern Spain are among the top table wines.

Portuguese wines — Although most Portuguese wines are better known locally, three wine families have gained world prominence — Port, Madeira, and Rosé. Port, a dessert wine, must be produced within the Douro region. Madeira wine, also a dessert wine, gets its name from its homeland, the Portuguese-owned island of Madeira. Portuguese Rośe wines are often sold in earthenware bottles.

United States-produced wines: America's wineries market generic, varietal, and proprietary wines. The federal government and, in some cases, the state governments strictly control the production, naming, and selling of these wines. Generally, the wines are categorized into two major geographical divisions: Californian wines and American wines (wines produced in any other state).

Californian wines — Eighty percent of America's wines are produced in California. Because of climatic conditions unique to California, virtually every European grape variety can be successfully cultivated there. Thus, California offers a large number of wines.

American wines — About 11 percent of the United States' wines are produced in the northern New York area known as the Finger Lakes region. The remaining nine percent come from many other states such as Ohio and Michigan. Eastern wineries rely mainly on the native

---

How wines are named

The name of a wine can be recognized as falling into one of the three main categories: generic, varietal, or proprietary.

The generic wine names usually are the oldest and most well-known ones. These names frequently, but not always, identify the European region, commune, city, or vineyard where the wines were first made.

Generic Name	Geographical Origin
Burgundy	Burgundy region of France
Port	City of Oporto, Portugal
Claret	Bordeaux region of France
Sherry	City of Jerez, Spain

Wines with characteristics similar to these Old World wines but made in other parts of the world may also be given generic names. The generic name must be accompanied by the place where the wine was made.

Generic Name	Wine Name With Origin
Sherry	California Sherry
Champagne	New York Champagne
Chablis	American Chablis

Varietal naming, a second method of naming wines, is particularly popular in the United States. The name of a varietal wine identifies the major grape variety (by United States law, at least 51 percent) that is used in making the wine. Some varietal wines are blends of several grape varieties, with one grape variety predominating; others are made from only one grape variety. Quite often, a varietal wine will have appearance and taste characteristics similar to those of a wine that is generically named.

Generic	Varietal Counterpart
Claret	Cabernet Sauvignon, Zinfandel
Rhine	Riesling, Sylvaner
Chablis	Pinot Chardonnay, Pinot Blanc

The proprietary name, a third type of wine nomenclature, often is given to a special wine that has unique character and is made by only one vintner or winery. Rubion, Paisano, Capella, Vins da Tovora, and Emerald Dry are examples of such names.

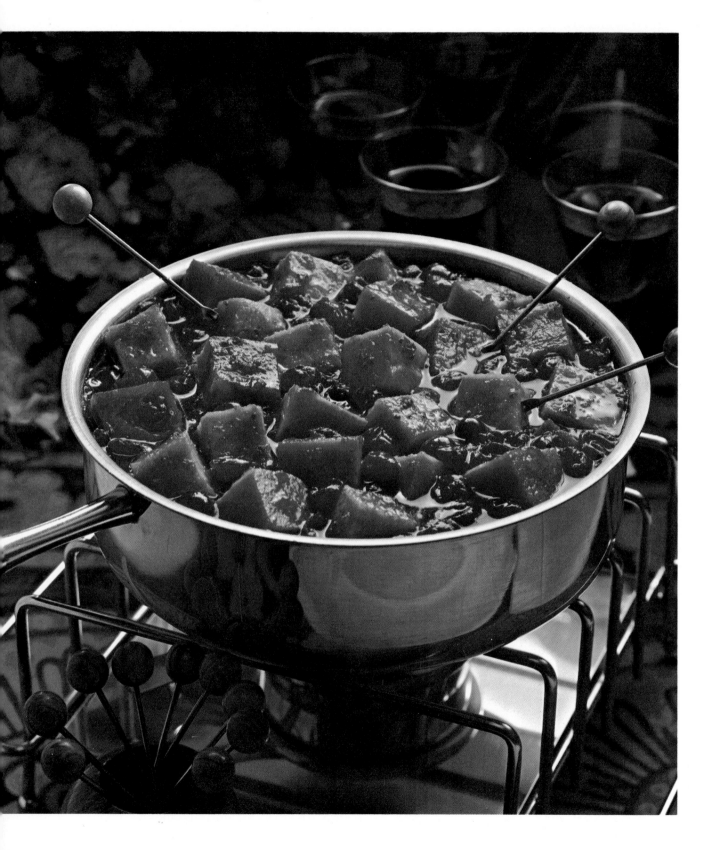

American grapes and their hybrids, such as Delaware, Dutchess, and Niagara, for the varietal and generic wines.

How to select wines: What kind, how much, and what quality are three questions you need to answer before you buy wine. If you're new to the wine world, a wine label will help you quite a lot. The label not only indicates the brand name and descriptive name of the wine but also its origin and vintner, alcoholic content, net contents, and sometimes vintage year and how the wine is best used.

The statement of origin and vintner indicates where and by whom the wine was made. The origin may be very general (American Sherry) or be more specific, naming the state or region where the wine originated. The vintner's name and address must always be stated. "Estate bottled" may be used when the bottler produced wine from grapes grown in vineyards that are in the vicinity of the winery and are owned or controlled by the bottler. When three-fourths of the wine is produced by the vintner, it may be labeled "produced and bottled by" or "bottled at the winery." The phrase "made by" may indicate that the wine was bottled from a blend of wines made by more than one vintner.

The alcoholic content (always given by volume, never by proof) must be labeled on any wine containing 14 percent or more alcohol. If it has less than 14 percent alcohol, the wine must be denoted as "dinner," "light," or "table" wine *or* the alcoholic content must be stated.

The most common bottle size for United States' wines (irregardless of the shape) is the fifth. This has a net content of four-fifths quart or 25.6 ounces. Smaller and larger bottles are also available as needed. To judge how much wine you need, see the box on page 2472.

Appetizer openers

← Cranberry-Wine Hors d'Oeuvres, cubes of ham, chicken, and turkey that have simmered in a wine sauce, are for company.

A vintage year is rarely designated on United States' wines since the quality of the wines is consistent year after year. But all United States' wines so designated must have been produced within the specified year. European wine quality fluctuates more widely. Most of the vintage-dated European wines consist of wine produced in that year, although a small amount of wine produced in other than the vintage year may be included.

Last but not least, the label may indicate wine classification. Although this is not mandatory, wineries include the class, and often how to use the wine, as a guide to selection for consumers.

There are several points to consider when selecting a quality wine. A brand that has been produced for many years is probably one you can rely on. And, in general, the more specific the wine name, the better the quality. A domestic wine named Riesling, for instance, is produced under more rigid controls than the generic one called Rhine wine. The bottler's statement, "estate bottled," is a more exact designation of the wine's source than "produced by" and "made by."

How to store wines: Since wine continues to change after it is bottled, it is necessary to know a few storage guidelines to keep wine at its best.

Unopened corked bottles of wine should be stored on their sides, away from sunlight, at a constant temperature (ideally 55° to 60° and not over 70°), and free from vibrations. This permits the wine to age without spoiling. Screwcap bottles may be stored upright or on their sides.

You don't need an involved setup to meet wine storage needs. A wine rack as simple as a wine packing case placed on its side and located in a quiet place will do. If possible, arrange the bottles in the rack so that the less-stable wines are kept the coolest: sparkling and white dinner wines on the bottom, rosé and red table wines in the middle, and appetizer and dessert wines on top.

Storage for partially used bottles of wine is quite a separate story. Opened wines with over 14 percent alcohol may be refrigerator stored for weeks. However, because of the lower alcoholic content, dinner wines are more perishable when opened. Refrigerate the unused portion of dinner wines, tightly sealed, and use the remainder within a week to 10 days.

Sparkling wines are best served immediately after opening. If you have some left over, store it well-stoppered in the refrigerator and use in a day or two.

Unused portions of dinner or sparkling wine are not a loss. Besides being good beverages to accompany the meal, they are ideal for many cooking uses.

How to use wines: Although it's common knowledge that wines can be used as beverages or as ingredients in a wide variety of prepared foods, there are still many questions that arise concerning their use. At the outset, one thing must be clear. The guidelines that are given here are merely suggestions; they are not hard-and-fast rules. Wines are made to be enjoyed, and their use need not be tangled in a myriad of formalities.

As a beverage—You can serve wine as a beverage before, during, or after any meal course. Some of the suggested rules of etiquette used for selecting, opening, serving, and drinking wine follow.

First, there are guidelines that help in selecting the right wine for a certain course or a particular food. As with appetizer foods, appetizer wines are chosen to stimulate the appetite for the remaining courses of the meal. In this same light, sweet wines, like cakes and pies, are recommended for dessert.

Red and white dinner wines complement different types of foods. Usually robust, red wines pair well with hearty foods like beef, pork, cheese, and pasta dishes. The delicate white dinner wines, on the other hand, enhance subtly flavored foods—poultry, fish, or veal, for example—without overpowering the entrée.

Rosé and sparkling wines are enjoyed at all occasions by themselves or with any food. (For more specific wine-food pairing, see chart on page 2468.)

How Much Wine To Buy

The amounts of wine you need to buy are based on the average size of each wine serving. In the case of dinner and sparkling wines, the average serving is 4 to 6 ounces. For appetizer and dessert wines, figure on 2 to 2½ ounces per serving.

Bottle size	Fluid ounces	Number of servings	
		Dinner and sparkling wines	Appetizer and dessert wines
Split (2/5 pint)	6.4	2	2-3
Tenth (4/5 pint)	12.8	2-3	5-6
Pint	16	3-4	6-7
Fifth (4/5 quart)	25.6	4-6	10-12
Quart	32	5-8	12-16
Half gallon	64	10-16	25-32
Gallon	128	21-32	51-64

As with wine selection, recommendations for wine serving temperatures are helpful for the novice wine drinker. Most white and rosé wines are prechilled to between 45° and 50°, and sparkling wines are best even colder, 40° to 45°. Except for dry Sherry and dry Vermouth, which are chilled (45° to 55°) or served on the rocks, appetizer, dessert, and red dinner wines, for the most part, are served at a cool room temperature (60° to 70°). Red dinner wines are often opened about an hour before serving to allow the bouquet to develop more fully. Other wines are not opened until just before they are served.

Although there are many types of wineglasses, some with specific uses, the most important part is the wine, not the glass. The 8- to 10-ounce all-purpose wineglass that is clear, stemmed, and tulip-shaped is a good investment for multiple-use drinking. If you wish to add to your selection of glasses, the 6-ounce tulip glass is popular for appetizer and dessert wines. The tall, slender tulip or stemmed, saucerlike glass is good for sparkling wines.

Placement of wineglasses at the table is very simple: the wineglass is placed to the right and slightly ahead of the water glass. If there are to be two wines at the meal, place the glasses side-by-side or one in front of the other.

The proper use of a good corkscrew permits easy opening of a still wine bottle with a cork closure. For a still wine, cut the seal about ¼ inch below the bottle lip, remove the upper portion of the seal, then wipe the lip with a napkin. Insert the corkscrew. Giving a slight twist to the corkscrew as you begin to pull, remove the cork. Again using a napkin, wipe the inside of the bottle neck to remove any bits of remaining cork.

Uncorking sparkling wines requires care to prevent the cork from bursting out unexpectedly. First, cut the seal about 1½ inches down and remove the upper portion. Then, remove the wire hood by unwinding the loop. Keep your thumb on top of the cork as much as possible. With one hand holding the bottom portion of the bottle, grasp the cork with the other hand, keeping your thumb securely over the top of the cork. Angle the bottle to 45° (cork pointed away from you and anyone else) and begin twisting the bottle while holding the cork in a fixed position. As you twist, the internal bottle pressure will help push out the cork. Be sure to hold onto the cork as it leaves the bottle. If the cork doesn't come out, press the cork gently from side to side as you twist. Pour into glasses immediately.

When serving wine, make sure that the glasses are clean—completely dry and free of any film, lint, or water spots. The host first pours some wine into his glass and samples it. (In this way, he gets any pieces of cork, and an unpleasant wine can be detected.) After approving the wine, he pours the guests' glasses, filling a third to half full. Pour sparkling wine until the foam reaches the rim, then fill two-thirds to three-fourths full.

Tasting wine means taking in its color and bouquet, as well as its flavor. First, look at it for color, then sniff the bouquet. Take a sip and swirl the wine to the back of your tongue (that's where many taste buds are located). Hold it there a few seconds before swallowing. You will soon be using such descriptive words as fragrant, dry, sweet, and delicate to describe the taste sensations.

In addition to being served alone, wine also is used as an ingredient in mixed drinks and punches. Wines are well suited to this use since they contribute flavor and often color. They blend well with all kinds of fruit juices, carbonated beverages, sherbets, and ice creams.

Drier drinks such as Tomato-Vermouth Cocktail and Rosé Frappé are appetite stimulants. Sweeter versions such as Sherried Chocolate Frappé better fit into the refreshment and dessert uses.

Tomato-Vermouth Cocktail

2 cups tomato juice, chilled
½ cup dry vermouth
1 tablespoon lemon juice
   Ice

Combine all ingredients in shaker or screw-top jar; adjust lid. Shake well and chill. Serve in small glasses with ice. Serves 4.

Burgundy and Sherry work together to flavor the meat for Beef à la Wellington. Liverwurst and pastry layers enwrap the beef.

Rosé Frappé

1 fifth rosé wine
1 6-ounce can frozen lemonade
   concentrate, thawed
¾ cup water

Stir together wine, lemonade concentrate, and water. Pour over crushed ice in sherbets to serve. Makes 8 servings.

Sherried Chocolate Frappé

2 cups milk
⅓ cup chocolate syrup
⅓ cup cream sherry
1 pint vanilla ice cream
• • •
Ground cinnamon

Combine milk, chocolate syrup, and sherry. Spoon ice cream into 4 tall glasses; pour chocolate mixture over. Muddle mixture slightly; sprinkle with cinnamon. Makes 4 servings.

Punches take on a special entertaining light when sparked with wine. Burgundy helps to give Ruby Wine Punch its color.

Ruby Wine Punch

¾ cup water
¾ cup sugar
6 inches stick cinnamon
1 teaspoon whole cloves
   Dash salt
2 cups red Burgundy, chilled
1 32-ounce bottle cranberry-
   apple juice, chilled

In saucepan combine first 5 ingredients; bring to boil. Reduce heat; simmer 10 minutes. Strain; chill liquid. Combine with wine and fruit juice. Makes 12 to 14 four-ounce servings.

As an ingredient — Probably no other food is more closely linked with gourmet cooking than is wine. A few dashes of wine added to an appetizer, entrée, or dessert seem to transform the food magically into a connoisseur's delight. Because wine can change the nature of a food dramatically, one might also think that it requires the hand of an adept cook. Yet, because of wine's versatility, nothing is easier than cooking with wine. In most cases, wines can be used interchangeably in foods. Furthermore, the flavors of most foods are enhanced by wine.

Just as with using herbs and spices, there are general suggestions that help you get the most enjoyment from seasoning foods with wines. But let your imagination be the most influential guide. For example, when a recipe calls for water, milk, or bouillon, consider substituting some wine for a portion of the liquid. If you've tried a recipe once with Sherry, the next time give it a different flavor twist by using Sauterne or another type of white wine. Instead of using red Burgundy, utilize another red wine or even a white or rosé wine. Each time you'll have created a new combination.

Although any sound wine can be used for cooking, a good wine with full body and distinctive flavor imparts the best cooking qualities. If you have some wine left from a meal or if you will be serving the wine at the meal to come, it's logical to use a little of it to flavor the food.

A wine designated as a "cooking wine" can be used equally well. The wine label will specify whether or not salt has been added to the wine. The seasoning level of the food may need to be adjusted when using a "salted" cooking wine.

Always use wine sparingly in food—you can always add more if it's needed. For best results, allow the natural flavor of the food to predominate.

Wine charts, besides being beverage guidelines, also are helpful when you cook with wine. For example, red dinner wines are more often used in hearty entrées; white dinner wines, in delicate-flavored entrees; and dessert wines, in dessert foods. Except when poured over fruit for an appetizer or dessert, sparkling wines do not serve a purpose in cooking since they lose one of their appeals, the effervescence.

Appetizer uses for wines encompass soups, canapés, dips, and hors d'oeuvres. Dry wine used in cheese fondue is a tradition. Onion soup takes on a new flair with a little white wine. Meat cube hors d'oeuvres boast a cranberry-wine sauce.

Onion-Wine Soup

In saucepan cook 3 medium onions, thinly sliced, in ¼ cup butter or margarine till lightly browned. Add two 10½-ounce cans *condensed* chicken broth, 1⅓ cups water, and ½ cup dry white wine; heat. Ladle into soup bowls. Sprinkle 8 toasted French bread slices with grated Parmesan cheese; float atop soup. Pass additional cheese, if desired. Makes 8 servings.

Cranberry-Wine Hors d'Oeuvres

    1 cup sugar
    ¾ cup water
    2 cups fresh cranberries
    ¼ cup dry white wine
    ¼ cup catsup
      Fully cooked ham, chicken, and
        turkey, cubed

In large saucepan combine sugar and water. Heat to boiling, stirring till sugar dissolves. Boil 5 minutes. Add cranberries; cook till skins pop, 5 minutes. Remove from heat. Stir in wine and catsup. Pour into small blazer pan of chafing dish; place meat in sauce. Keep warm over hot water (bain-marie). Spear with cocktail picks. Makes 2 cups sauce.

Wine gives gourmet flavor to meats and fishes of all kinds. As when drinking wines, red wines are often teamed with red meats and white wines with white meats. With fish, shellfish, and game meats, wine subdues intense flavors.

Beef à la Wellington

    1 cup red Burgundy
    1 cup dry sherry
    1 onion, quartered
    2 bay leaves
    1 3-pound eye of round beef roast
    2 cups sifted all-purpose flour
  ⅔ cup shortening
    1 4¾-ounce can liverwurst spread
    1 slightly beaten egg
    3 tablespoons all-purpose flour

Combine the first 4 ingredients. Place meat in pan; pour marinade over. Cover; refrigerate overnight. Remove meat from marinade, reserving ¼ cup for gravy. Roast meat on rack in shallow roasting pan at 425° till meat thermometer registers 130°, about 1¼ hours. Reserve drippings. Cool the meat.

Sift together 2 cups flour and ½ teaspoon salt; cut in shortening till coarse crumbs. Gradually add ⅓ to ½ cup cold water, tossing with fork till dampened. Form into ball. Roll to 12x11-inch rectangle; spread with liverwurst to within ½ inch of edges. Place meat, top side down, in center of pastry. Draw up long sides to overlap. Brush with egg to seal. Trim ends; fold up and brush with more egg to seal.

Place on greased baking sheet, seam side down. Brush with remaining egg. Bake at 425° for 30 to 35 minutes. Heat ¾ cup water with drippings. Blend together the 3 tablespoons flour and ½ cup cold water; add to pan with marinade. Cook, stirring constantly, till bubbly. Season to taste. Serves 8 to 12.

Wine flavor in a main dish comes from using the wine as a marinade, a basting sauce, or in a sauce. A marinade serves a dual purpose—it adds flavor and helps to tenderize less-tender cuts of meat.

Beef with Wine Sauce

1 pound ground beef
½ cup rosé wine
1½ teaspoons cornstarch
1 tablespoon lemon juice
¼ cup orange marmalade

Form meat into 4 patties about ¾ inch thick. Sprinkle with salt. Broil 3 to 4 inches from heat for 6 minutes. Turn; broil 4 minutes longer or to desired degree of doneness.

Meanwhile, in small saucepan blend wine with cornstarch. Stir in lemon juice and marmalade. Cook, stirring constantly, till mixture thickens and bubbles. To serve, garnish patties with orange slices, if desired. Spoon wine sauce atop. Makes 4 servings.

Scallopine Burgers

1½ pounds ground veal
1 cup soft bread crumbs
1 beaten egg
2 tablespoons milk
¼ cup all-purpose flour
¼ cup salad oil
1 8-ounce can tomato sauce
1 3-ounce can chopped mushrooms, undrained
¼ cup dry white wine
1 tablespoon finely snipped parsley
¼ teaspoon dried oregano leaves, crushed
Hot cooked noodles
Grated Parmesan cheese

Combine veal, crumbs, egg, milk, ½ teaspoon salt, and dash pepper; shape into 6 patties. Coat lightly with ¼ cup all-purpose flour. Brown in hot oil in skillet. Drain off excess fat. Combine tomato sauce, undrained mushrooms, wine, parsley, and oregano; pour over meat. Cover; simmer 20 to 25 minutes. Serve on noodles; sprinkle with cheese. Serves 6.

Vegetables and salads take on elegance with the addition of wine, too. Add wine to a cream sauce for vegetables and to the gelatin for molded salads or to creamy salad dressings for tossed salads. Use white wines for light-colored gelatins, red wines for red-colored gelatins. Use wine vinegar in place of cider vinegar to create flavorful salad dressings.

Orange-Port Mold

2 3-ounce packages black cherry-flavored gelatin
1½ cups boiling water
3 oranges
1 cup port
1 cup orange juice

Dissolve cherry gelatin in the boiling water. Peel oranges; section each, reserving juice, and cut up pulp. Add enough water to reserved juice to make ½ cup liquid. Stir into dissolved gelatin along with wine and the additional 1 cup orange juice. Chill gelatin mixture till partially set. Fold in cut-up oranges; pour mixture into a 6½-cup ring mold. Chill till firm; unmold and fill center of ring with lettuce, if desired. Makes 8 to 10 servings.

To round out the recipe uses for wines, there is nothing more glamorous than wine-flavored desserts. Fruit compotes, dessert sauces, pies, and cakes become sophisticated food fare when spiced with an interesting wine.

Hot Fruit Compote

1 16-ounce package dried prunes
1⅓ cups dried apricots
1 13½-ounce can pineapple chunks, undrained (1⅔ cups)
1 21-ounce can cherry pie filling
2 cups water
¼ cup dry white wine

Arrange first three fruits in 9x9x2-inch baking dish. Combine pie filling, water, and wine; pour over fruit. Cover; bake at 350° for 1½ hours. Serve warm. Makes 8 servings.

Spirits

Fermented liquids have been distilled since before the Christian Era. The early Chinese distilled a spirit from rice beer. East Indians distilled fermented sugarcane and rice as early as 800 B.C.

The development of distilled spirits in Europe and the United States was influenced mostly by the Celts of Great Britain and by the Arabs of the Middle East. The Celts distilled the first whiskey-like liquor, which they called *uisgebaugh* (water of life). As the civilization of Great Britain progressed, this spirit evolved into the Scotch and Irish whiskies. Although the Arabs could not distill alcohol because of religious beliefs, they did coin the word alcohol and become proficient in the distillation of flower fragrances for perfumes. The Spanish adapted this process to the distillation of grape wine.

In Europe, the interest in drinking spirits developed during medieval times. France imposed heavy taxes, determined by volume, on exported wines. To reduce the tax and also to save on shipping costs, winegrowers began distilling wine into brandy. When imported, the alcohol was to be diluted to its original state. Instead, the distilled product was soon recognized as being palatable itself.

Rum and later grain spirits were the most-consumed spirits in early America. It became more economical to ship grain grown in western Pennsylvania and Kentucky as spirits than as fresh grains. Distilleries sprang up on many farms.

Besides the traditional grain whiskies, one new type, named Bourbon after the Kentucky county where it was first made, was developed by an inventive distiller. The demand for Bourbon and other Kentucky whiskies sparked the growth of a new industry. Today, Kentucky distills 70 percent of American-produced spirits.

How spirits are produced: The distillation of alcohol from a fermented liquid (called the mash) is based on the fact that alcohol boils at a lower temperature than water (about 175° versus 212°). Wines, sugarcane, molasses, and grains are some of the raw materials used for the mash.

What is "proof?"

In times past, the strength of a liquor was determined by mixing equal portions of the liquor with gunpowder and igniting them. If the gunpowder did not burn, the spirit was too weak. If the flame was overly bright, the spirit was too strong. A spirit that created an even, blue flame, however, was said to have been "proved."

Today, the strength of a distilled alcohol is called its proof. Each degree of proof is equivalent to a half-percent of alcohol. Thus, a spirit that is labeled 160 proof consists of 80 percent alcohol.

When the liquid is heated to around 200° (boiling), the alcohol vaporizes; the water is left behind. This vapor is condensed in a closed container. It is now a highly alcoholic liquid – a spirit.

In theory, if all the alcohol is separated, the liquid will be completely pure – 200 proof, colorless, odorless, and tasteless. In actuality, however, the purest spirits available, called neutral spirits, are distilled at 190 proof.

The apparatus used in the production of spirits is commonly referred to as a still. There are two kinds of stills – the older (but still used) is the batch still; the newer is called a continuous still. Although the batch still frequently produces a more flavorful product, distillation must be repeated two or three times to achieve the desired purity and alcoholic strength. The continuous still, on the other hand, requires no redistillation.

If the fermented liquid is distilled to less than 190 proof (which is most often the case), other substances in the liquid rise off with the alcohol. These elements, known as congeners, are the flavor components that develop during the aging process of a liquor. When aged in wood, the congeners create the characteristic appearance, aroma, and taste of the particular spirit. The lower the proof at which a spirit is distilled, the more congeners that are present in the alcohol and the more character the spirit has.

Not all of the spirits attain their flavors and appearances by wood-aging. Some, such as gin, are simply neutral spirits that have been distilled with flavoring components such as herbs.

After the desired aging has taken place, the spirit is bottled. Once it is in sealed glass containers, the spirit no longer changes in character.

Types of spirits: Varying the kind of fermented liquid used as well as the aging, flavoring, and blending techniques enables the production of many different spirits. The wide variety available suit the wide range of taste preferences.

Brandy is usually the distilled product of grape wine, but it may also be the distillate of other fruit wines. Except for grape brandy, the fruits from which the brandies are made (apple, cherry, for example) must be specified on the labels.

Liquors labeled "fruit-flavored" brandies, common to United States' markets, are not true fruit brandies. In reality, they are liqueurs consisting of grape brandy to which fruit flavors have been infused and sugar syrup added.

Gin is based on diluted neutral spirits that are distilled and sometimes redistilled in the presence of flavoring components. The traditional but not the only flavoring ingredient is juniper berries. Most gin is unaged, which results in a clear, colorless spirit.

Liqueur, also called cordial, is the family name for certain sweet, after-dinner spirits. Usually based on either neutral spirits or brandy, liqueurs are flavored by infusing or distilling the flavoring agents (plant flowers, roots, seeds, fruits, and the like) with the spirits.

Rum is distilled from sugarcane or molasses mash. For the most part, the dark rums are aged longer and have more intense flavor than the light rums.

Blazing entrée

← Warmed brandy provides the glowing flame for the pineapple- and apricot-sauced breasts of chicken in delicious Chicken Fantasia.

Tequila, Mexico's national drink, is a colorless spirit distilled from the fermented mash of the maguey plant.

Vodka has the least identifiable flavor of any spirit because it is simply diluted neutral spirits. No flavorings are added. Although often thought to be a potato distillate, vodka is more often distilled from grain or any inexpensive food.

Whiskey, although basically a grain distillate, comes in assorted types, depending on where, from what, and how it is made. All whiskies are aged in wood, usually oak. Scotch, Irish, and Canadian whiskies are made in the countries for which they are named. Each has a unique flavor—smoky, full-bodied, and light-bodied respectively. Of the many United States whiskies, the most all-American is Bourbon, made mainly from corn.

How to select and store spirits: When selecting spirits, purchase according to its intended use or your personal brand preferences. The superior-quality spirits are enjoyed by most people when they are consumed straight, over ice, or in cocktails of low dilution. For punches and more diluted cocktails, a less-expensive spirit usually suits the purpose adequately. Because production costs are passed on to the consumer, price is usually the best indication of quality.

Spirits are most often sold in fifths and quarts, but half-pints and pints are suitable for small use. Half-gallons are economical buys for large parties.

Because spirits are stable once they are bottled, most of them can be shelf stored for long periods. However, opened bottles of liqueurs lose their flavor power with storage. Pints of liqueurs are frequently most practical for home use.

How to use spirits: Spirits are America's traditional ingredients for cocktails and other alcoholic beverages, but they can also add new dimensions to prepared dishes. Using these beverage and cooking techniques will help you to develop a method of creating flavorful foods.

As a beverage—Efficient mixing and serving of spiritous beverages is one of the marks of a good host or hostess. First, master the drinks you and your friends like best, then add a new drink to your repertoire from time to time. To make flavorful drinks you need the proper supplies: spirits and nonalcoholic accompaniments, bar supplies, and glassware.

The supply of spirits and drink accompaniments that you need depends on what drinks you plan to serve. Carbonated beverages such as club soda, ginger ale, and quinine water are common mixers. When fruit juices are needed for drinks, juice squeezed from fresh fruits imparts the best flavor. You may also need bitters and garnishes such as orange or lemon slices, maraschino cherries, and cocktail olives and onions. Since alcohol and icy liquids are poor solvents for sugar, fine granulated sugar (not confectioners') or a simple syrup are used for sweetening.

Simple Syrup

Combine equal amounts of sugar and water. Boil for 5 minutes. Store in a covered jar in the refrigerator until it is needed.

For bar equipment you can make use of kitchen items that you already own, but you will also need some special tools. Kitchen supplies that move to the bar include bottle openers, corkscrew, paring knife, juice strainer, ice cube cracker, ice crusher, ice bucket, and tongs. You'll probably also want coasters, straws, and cocktail napkins. Special bar supplies that you may have to purchase are the bar spoon, jigger-pony measure, bar strainer, and a mixer-shaker or blender.

Mixed drinks look best in specially designed glassware. Stemmed 4- to 6-ounce cocktail glasses are ideal for the ice cold but iceless cocktails. Stemless old-fashioned glasses with 7- to 8-ounce capacity are best for on-the-rocks drinks. The all-purpose wineglass can be used for any of the sours, Bloody Marys, or other medium-sized drinks. Tall highball glasses (8 to 12 ounces) are for large drinks such as highballs and Collins. And for liqueurs, the ¾- to 1-ounce cordial glasses are most appropriate.

Common bar measurements

1 wineglass equals 4 ounces
1 jigger equals 1½ ounces or 3 tablespoons
1 pony equals 1 ounce
1 ounce equals 2 tablespoons
1 dash equals ⅙ teaspoon
Juice of 1 lime is about 1 tablespoon
Juice of 1 lemon is about 3 tablespoons
1 bar spoon equals 1 teaspoon or ⅛ ounce

For good-tasting drinks, accurate measuring of ingredients is most important. Icing the drink without overdiluting it is equally vital. When you mix the ingredients, remember the following tips:

1. Prechill all of the ingredients and the glasses ahead of time.

2. The more ice used in the shaker, the faster the cooling of the liquid and the less the dilution of the beverage.

3. Do not overstir or overshake. This mistake results in excess dilution.

4. For faster chilling of on-the-rocks drinks, always use cracked ice.

5. If you use a blender for mixing, prechill the blender container and blend the ingredients for only a few seconds.

6. Before serving, add an appealing garnish if one suits the drink.

Warren's Glugg

Serve the punch informally right from the kettle—

Combine 2 quarts apple juice; ½ pound light raisins; 3 sticks cinnamon, broken; 1 tablespoon whole cloves; 4 cardamom buds;* and dash ground nutmeg. Let mixture stand for 12 to 24 hours. Before serving, pour the mixture into a kettle and bring to boiling; reduce heat and simmer for 30 minutes. Add 1½ oranges, sliced and quartered; heat through. Add 1 fifth dark rum and 1 fifth brandy. Serve mixture immediately from kettle; keep warm over low heat. Makes about 24 punch cup servings.

*Use seeds only from cardamom buds; shell and crush the seeds between two tablespoons or in a mortar and pestle. Steep the crushed seeds in 2 or 3 tablespoons boiling water.

Tonic

Use gin, vodka, or Tequila—

Combine juice and rind of ¼ lime, 1 jigger gin, vodka, *or* Tequila (1½ ounces), and ice cubes in tall glass. Fill with tonic water. Stir.

As an ingredient—Since the function of a spirit as an ingredient is to flavor food, it is important to know how to use it and pair it with different foods.

Because excess alcohol imparts harsh flavor, moderation is the foremost guide to adding spirits to foods. Uncooked dishes rapidly take on the alcohol undertones. For cooked dishes, heat the mixture until the alcohol evaporates. The remaining spirit flavor should enhance but not overpower the flavor of the food.

For great drama, flame the added spirits. First, the spirit must have a sufficient concentration of alcohol. Spirits higher than 70 proof are best. If you use a liquor of low proof, add some vodka or brandy to increase the alcoholic strength. Next, place the liquor in a small saucepan and warm slowly till the alcohol begins to vaporize. Do not overheat. At the table, ignite the warmed alcohol (either in the saucepan or poured into a ladle), using a

Irish Coffee Pie (see *Pie* for recipe) is a dessert rendition of the famed beverage. The coffee- and whiskey-flavored filling is garnished with whipped cream and shaved chocolate.

safety match, and pour the flaming liquid over the dish. Allow the fire to burn out naturally. Although the technique appears to require a deft hand, you, too, can easily master this cooking art.

Banana-Raspberry Flambé

    1 10-ounce package frozen
      raspberries, thawed
    6 tablespoons orange liqueur
    2 tablespoons granulated sugar
    3 tablespoons butter or margarine
    1 tablespoon brown sugar
    6 medium bananas, sliced

Banana-Raspberry Flambé features an orange liqueur-sparked fruit sauce that is flamed and spooned over scoops of ice cream.

Combine raspberries, *2 tablespoons* liqueur, and granulated sugar in blender container. Cover; blend till smooth. Sieve. In blazer pan of chafing dish melt butter; add brown sugar. When sugar is dissolved, add bananas. Cook 2 to 3 minutes. Add raspberry mixture to bananas; heat through. Heat remaining liqueur in ladle or small saucepan; flame and pour over fruits. Serve over ice cream. Makes 4 cups.

The pairing of spirits with food follows that for wines — full-bodied spirits season hearty foods well, while light-bodied spirits team better with delicate foods. Because of its lack of flavor, vodka does not serve a special cooking purpose.

Brandy sparks appetizer dips and spreads, meaty main dishes, coffee-flavored foods, puddings, cakes, and ice cream sauces. Fruit-flavored brandies are naturals with many fruit dishes.

Snow-Capped Pâté

    ½ cup chopped onion
    1 small clove garlic, crushed
    ¼ cup butter or margarine
    1 pound fresh or frozen chicken
      livers, thawed
    2 teaspoons all-purpose flour
    ¼ teaspoon salt
    ¼ teaspoon dried thyme leaves,
      crushed
      Dash pepper
    4 teaspoons brandy
    2 3-ounce packages cream cheese,
      cubed and softened
    3 tablespoons milk
    ¼ cup snipped parsley
    ½ cup chopped pecans

Cook onion and garlic in butter till tender. Add livers; cook, covered, 7 to 8 minutes. Stir in flour, salt, thyme, and pepper. Add brandy; cook and stir 1 minute. Transfer to blender container. Cover; blend smooth. (When necessary, use rubber spatula to scrape down sides.) Mold in small greased bowl; chill.

Unmold. Add cream cheese and milk to blender container. Cover; blend smooth. Spread over mold. Chill till serving time. Sprinkle parsley and nuts atop pâté. Serve with crackers.

Chicken Fantasia

    6 small chicken breasts, boned
        and skinned (about 2½ pounds)
    6 thin slices boiled ham
    2 tablespoons butter or margarine
    ½ cup apricot preserves
    2 tablespoons vinegar
    ½ teaspoon salt
    ½ teaspoon dry mustard
    1 8¾-ounce can pineapple tidbits
    2 tablespoons cornstarch
    ¼ cup brandy

Place chicken, boned side up, on cutting board. Pound to make cutlets ¼ inch thick. Place a ham slice on each cutlet; tuck in sides and roll up jelly-roll fashion. Skewer or tie. In large skillet slowly brown chicken in butter. Stir in ⅔ cup water, preserves, vinegar, salt, and mustard. Cook, covered, 20 minutes.

Drain pineapple, reserving syrup. Blend cornstarch and reserved syrup. Stir cornstarch mixture and pineapple tidbits into sauce in skillet. Cook, uncovered, till chicken is tender, 15 minutes, turning chicken rolls once.

At serving time, transfer chicken to blazer pan of chafing dish; garnish with canned apricot halves, if desired. Place over chafing dish burner. Pour sauce into heatproof dish. In small saucepan warm brandy; at table pour brandy over sauce. Ignite immediately; spoon flaming sauce over chicken. Makes 6 servings.

Hamburger Steak Diane

    1½ pounds ground round or sirloin
    1 teaspoon dry mustard
    2 tablespoons butter or margarine
    1 to 2 tablespoons lemon juice
    1 tablespoon snipped parsley
    ½ teaspoon Worcestershire sauce
    ¼ cup brandy

Combine meat, mustard, 1 teaspoon salt, and dash pepper; mix well. Shape into 5 patties, ½ inch thick. Melt butter in blazer pan of chafing dish over direct heat. Cook 2 minutes on each side; remove. To blazer pan add lemon juice, parsley, and Worcestershire; bring to boiling. Reduce heat. In saucepan heat brandy over very low heat. Pour brandy over sauce; ignite. Serve at once over meat. Serves 5.

Bourbon adds a different touch to barbecue sauces and chocolate desserts. Bourbon Balls are a good confection.

Bourbon Balls

    60 vanilla wafers
    ½ cup walnuts
    1 cup sifted confectioners' sugar
    2 tablespoons unsweetened cocoa
        powder
    ¼ cup bourbon
    ¼ cup light corn syrup
        Granulated sugar

Break 6 wafers into blender; blend to fine crumbs. Repeat. Put nuts in blender; blend till chopped. Add to crumbs. Combine confectioners' sugar, cocoa, and crumbs. Stir in bourbon and corn syrup. If necessary, add 1¼ teaspoons water so that mixture will shape. Form into ¾-inch balls. Roll in granulated sugar. Store in covered container. Makes 48.

Rum is one of the best seasonings for use in tropical foods such as chocolate, coffee, pineapple, and citrus fruits.

Orange-Rum Cake

    2 17-ounce packages pound
        cake mix
    2 tablespoons shredded orange
        peel
    2 teaspoons shredded lemon peel
    1 cup sugar
    1 cup orange juice
    3 tablespoons lemon juice
    2 tablespoons rum

Prepare cake mixes together according to package directions, adding fruit peel. Turn into greased and lightly floured 10-inch tube pan. Bake at 350° till done, 1 to 1¼ hours. Cool 10 minutes; remove from pan. Cool 20 minutes.

Place on serving plate. Using long-tined fork or skewer, punch holes in top of cake at 1-inch intervals. Combine remaining ingredients; bring to boiling. Spoon *very slowly* over cake, *a small amount at a time*, allowing cake to absorb sauce. Continue till syrup is used. Chill.

Probably the most versatile spirits for ingredient uses are the liqueurs with their vast range of flavors. Their intenseness again implies sparing use. Ideas for using liqueurs include spooning them as is over ice cream, sherbet, or fruit, or adding them to dessert sauces or dessert soufflés. Liqueurs, such as orange- and mint-flavored ones, also enhance duck, pork, lamb, and fish entrées when the sweetness of the liqueur is tempered by the addition of a little lemon juice.

Orange-Date Medley

Almond topping adds crunch—

> 5 oranges, peeled and sectioned
> 1 cup sliced, pitted dates
> 1 cup orange juice
> 2 tablespoons orange liqueur
> ¼ cup toasted, slivered almonds

Place orange sections and dates in 10x6x1½-inch baking dish. Combine orange juice and orange liqueur; pour over fruit. Bake, covered, at 350° till heated through, about 30 minutes. Sprinkle almonds over top. Serves 6.

Lime Fizz

Prechill glasses in the freezer—

> ¼ cup frozen limeade concentrate, thawed
> 3 ounces gin (2 jiggers)
> 2 teaspoons fine granulated sugar
> 2 teaspoons white crème de menthe
> 1 drop green food coloring
> 2 cups crushed ice
> 1 7-ounce bottle carbonated water, chilled
> Fresh mint leaves

In blender container combine limeade concentrate, gin, sugar, white crème de menthe, green food coloring, and ice; blend for a few seconds. Divide mixture evenly into two highball glasses. Fill with carbonated water. Stir gently with up-and-down motion. Trim with fresh mint leaves. Makes 2 servings.

WINTERGREEN—The aromatic flavor born by the leaves of an evergreen herb that is distributed widely in northern woods. The bright red berries are often called checkerberries and can be eaten.

Fresh wintergreen cannot be obtained unless you know where to gather it, but oil of wintergreen, an aromatic, volatile oil, is available at pharmacies for use in making candies and confections. The oil is potent, so a few drops are sufficient to carry the flavor through an entire batch of candy. (See also *Flavoring*.)

WINTER SQUASH—Any fully mature squash variety with a hard rind and seeds. The best-known varieties of winter squash are acorn, banana, butternut, delicious, hubbard, and turban squash.

In addition to being packed with vitamin A, these dark yellow vegetables also contribute a fair amount of the B vitamin riboflavin. One-half cup of baked winter squash provides about 65 calories.

Although there is a wide color and shape differential between varieties, in general, purchase winter squash that have hard rinds and good variety color and shape, and that are heavy for their size. Most winter squash are marketed during fall and winter, but their storage stability enables year-round availability. If stored in a cool, dry area, winter squash will maintain their quality for several months. Handle gently to prevent bruising or damaging, as decay will set in.

Unlike summer squash, the rinds and seeds of winter squash are not usually eaten. Bake small varieties whole or cut in half and bake with seasoned butter or a meat or vegetable stuffing. For large squash, cut in cubes or serving-sized pieces before cooking. (See also *Squash*.)

WIRE WHIP—Another name for the utensil called a whisk. (See also *Whisk*.)

WITLOOF CHICORY *(wit′ lōf)*—An alternate name for the vegetable Belgian Endive. (See also *Belgian Endive*.)

WOK—An iron, aluminum, or copper cooking pan of Chinese origin having a round bottom, sloping sides, and one or more

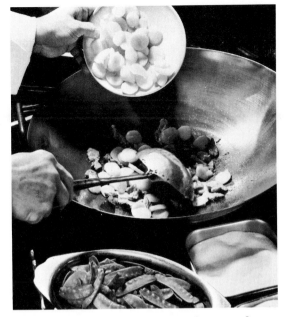

Try your hand at oriental cookery and prepare the main dish in a wok — a round, basin-shaped cooking pan of Chinese origin.

handles. Some woks have two handles, while others have one long handle, similar to that found on a frying pan. Modern versions usually are sold in a metal stand, which allows the pan to sit on the range without tipping. Pan sizes range from 10 inches to over 24 inches. The larger sizes are used mainly by restaurants.

The wok is used for stir-frying, braising, and stewing oriental dishes. Because of its shape, sauces or oil, if used, drains to the center where the heat is concentrated. Thus, quick cooking and constant stirring or tossing are necessary. It is an easy pan to keep clean because there are no corners in which the food can lodge. The wok should be seasoned before using. (See also *Oriental Cookery*.)

WON TON—The name of the Chinese filled dumpling. It is made of noodle dough with a meat, seafood, or vegetable filling, somewhat like a tiny ravioli. Won ton are served in broth for a soup, or they can be simmered in boiling water, fried, and served with a sauce. Won ton wrappers can be purchased in some specialty stores.

WOODRUFF—A perennial, wild herb. The leaves are long, oval, and deep green; the flowers are white. The dried leaves have a sweet aroma. Other names for this herb are sweet woodruff and waldmeister.

The most popular use of woodruff is to flavor the German punch, May wine. Woodruff also adds flavor to candies, punches, fruit cups, and other beverages.

WORCESTERSHIRE SAUCE (*wŏŏs' tuhr shēr,' -shuhr*)—A piquant brown liquid seasoning sauce that takes its name from Worcester, England, where it was first prepared commercially many years ago. Its ancestry, however, dates back to ancient India and to the Romans.

Worcestershire is commercially prepared by secret formula from soy sauce, anchovies, onions, tamarinds, garlic, vinegar, molasses, sugar, salt, and spices. It's a sauce for meats, but it is also used in sauces, soups, and casseroles.

Cheeseburger Pie

Combine 1 pound ground beef; ½ cup evaporated milk; ½ cup catsup; ⅓ cup fine dry bread crumbs; ¼ cup chopped onion; ¾ teaspoon salt; ½ teaspoon dried oregano leaves, crushed; and ⅛ teaspoon pepper. Prepare pastry for one-crust 8-inch pie (see *Pastry* for recipe). Line pie plate with pastry and fill with meat mixture. Bake at 350° for 35 to 40 minutes. Toss 4 ounces process American cheese, shredded (1 cup), with 1 teaspoon Worcestershire sauce. Sprinkle atop pie. Bake 10 minutes longer. Remove from oven; let stand 10 minutes before serving. Makes 6 servings.

WORMWOOD—A bitter herb used in making absinthe, a potent liqueur. The plant is native to Europe and northern Asia. Because absinthe made with wormwood is thought to have harmful effects on the nervous system, absinthe is outlawed in many countries, including the United States. Absinthe is still made in Spain.

WURST (*wûrst, wŏŏrst*)—The German word for sausage. The word is used alone or in a combined type name, such as liverwurst.

X-Y

XERES *(hā' rās)*—The French word for sherry wine, derived from Jerez, the name of the Spanish town where the wine originated.

YAM—1. A starchy root vegetable of the *Dioscorea* genus that is common to tropical regions. **2.** The name given to a moist-fleshed sweet potato.

The true *Dioscorea* yams have been a staple food of Central and South America for centuries. When Columbus and his fellow explorers landed at Haiti in 1492, they were given yams to eat by the natives. Later, African slaves from Senegal that were brought to the West Indies named these vegetables *nyami*, their word for "to eat." Yams were then taken back to Africa and cultivated there.

There are hundreds of varieties of true yams found and used abundantly in the southern regions of the Western Hemisphere. Some are immense, growing 7 to 8 feet in length and weighing over 100 pounds; others, called yampees, are smaller than a potato. In texture, they may be coarse, dry, and mealy; fine and tender; and crisp or mushy. Flavor varies.

True yams are seen in our country only as oddities, but in the tropics they are enjoyed in many dishes. Yams can be prepared in a variety of ways—baking, boiling, steaming, or frying.

The vegetables labeled yams in the supermarkets, on the other hand, are a type of sweet potato. They have brown skins with orange to pinkish orange overcasts and golden orange flesh that is sweet and syrupy when cooked. Louisiana and Florida are the primary producers of this vegetable. (See also *Sweet Potato*.)

YEAST—Microscopic, one-celled living plants. Yeast converts carbohydrates into alcohol and carbon dioxide gas; this process is known as fermentation.

Certain types of yeasts are used to bring about alcoholic fermentation in the production of wine and champagne and in the brewing of beer. Other yeasts provide leavening in raised bread products, resulting in a light, porous structure. Another type of yeast, brewers' yeast, is a dried yeast that is available in tablet or powdered form. It is consumed for its nutritional value.

Yeast is the earliest known leavening agent. It was used by the Egyptians for making beer and bread about 2000 B.C. The ancient Egyptians noted that when their bread dough was set aside, the mixture puffed up and soured—improving the flavor. Unknown to them, yeast plants from the air settled on the dough and grew into the dough. With this newly discovered bread product, the Egyptians invented an oven in which to bake the puffy bread. They also noticed that a piece of the dough from a previous batch could be used to leaven the next freshly made batch of dough. In this way, the first leavened sour dough bread came into being. However, it wasn't until the late nineteenth century that the details of yeast chemistry were discovered.

From this early method of leavening bread, a much more satisfactory way was discovered to grow the yeast for breadmaking. At one time, yeast was grown on mashes used in brewing beer. In the late eighteenth century, an Englishman discovered how to compress yeast.

Years later, in 1868, an American, Charles Fleischmann, introduced an improved yeast that was pressed into cakes. This made it possible for breadmaking to be carried out commercially on a large scale. In the years that followed, yeasts were improved by dehydration, forming another product called active dry yeast. This dry form originally was made for the military so that fresh bread could be made on the battlefield. Later improvements of active dry yeast included finer granules, which make for easier blending of the yeast with other ingredients.

Certain conditions are necessary for good yeast growth. Yeast grows best at warm temperatures—80° to 90° F. With temperatures that are higher than this, there is a possibility of killing the yeast. At lower temperatures, the action of the yeast is slowed down.

Yeast also needs carbohydrates, such as sugar, and moisture to live and bring about the fermentation action. During

Choose from an assortment of breads leavened with yeast. They include Refrigerated Herb Rolls, round Sweet Banana Bread, Cream of Potato Soup Bread, Two-Tone Bread, Cheese Braid.

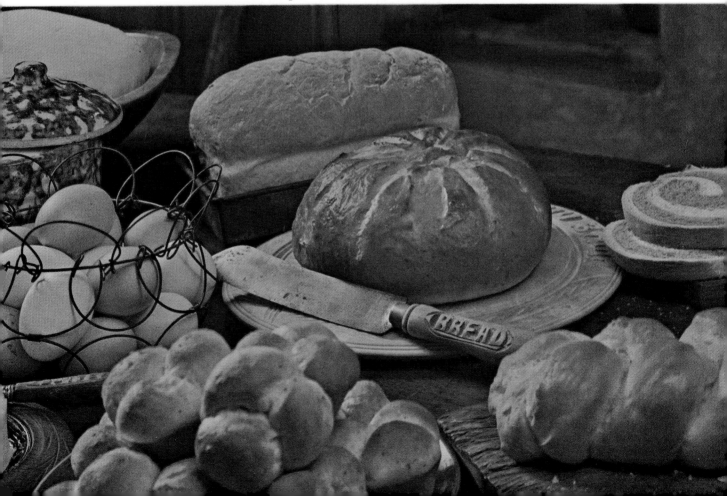

fermentation, the enzymes present in the yeast break down the carbohydrate in the warm, moist dough, producing bubbles of carbon dioxide gas. These gas bubbles are trapped in the dough as the bread bakes. Alcohol that forms during fermentation is driven off during baking.

Yeast products available to homemakers for baking purposes include compressed cakes and active dry yeast. Both of these yeasts are alive in their packages; however, the active dry yeast is in a resting stage until suspended in warm liquid. It should be dissolved in warm water or mixed with part of the flour.

Active dry yeast and compressed yeast can be substituted for one another since one cake of compressed yeast equals one package or about two teaspoons active dry yeast. Follow label or recipe directions for the method of dissolving and incorporating the type of yeast being used.

Compressed yeast is a mixture of yeast and a small amount of starch. It is perishable and must be kept under refrigeration. If you question whether the yeast is still usable, crumble it between your fingers. If it crumbles easily, it is still good. It is desirable to dissolve compressed yeast in lukewarm water (about 85° F).

The more popular type of yeast used by homemakers for baking bread is the active dry yeast, which is sold in moisture-proof, airtight packages or vacuum-packed jars. It can be stored on the shelf in a cool place for several months. Be sure to use the yeast before the expiration date stamped on the package. To lengthen the storage time of active dry yeast, store it in the refrigerator.

There are several methods of adding yeast to the other ingredients when making bread products. The most recent technique involves combining active dry yeast with a portion of the flour. The liquid and some of the other ingredients are heated together and added to the dry mixture. Then, the eggs are added. An electric mixer is used to beat the dough at this stage, then the remaining flour is stirred in by hand.

Another mixing method that is used quite often calls for dissolving the yeast in either warm or lukewarm water. Then, the dissolved yeast is added to other combined ingredients and all of the flour is stirred in by hand.

Yeast is used to leaven many bread products, from plain white bread to coffee cakes. Rolls are another popular yeast bread. (See *Bread, Leavening Agent* for additional information.)

Two-Tone Bread

    2 packages active dry yeast
5¼ to 5½ cups sifted all-purpose
      flour
    3 cups milk
    ⅓ cup sugar
    ⅓ cup shortening
    1 tablespoon salt
    3 tablespoons dark molasses
2¼ cups whole wheat flour

In large mixer bowl combine the 2 packages yeast and *3 cups* of the all-purpose flour. Heat together milk, sugar, shortening, and salt just till warm, stirring occasionally to melt shortening. Add to dry ingredients in mixer bowl. Beat at low speed of electric mixer for ½ minute, scraping sides of bowl constantly. Beat 3 minutes at high speed.

Divide dough in half. To one half, stir in enough of the remaining all-purpose flour to make a moderately stiff dough. Turn onto lightly floured surface and knead till smooth and elastic, 5 to 8 minutes. Place in well-greased bowl, turning once to grease surface; set aside. To remaining dough, stir in molasses and whole wheat flour. Turn onto lightly floured surface. Knead till smooth and elastic, 5 to 8 minutes, kneading in enough additional all-purpose flour (about 3 tablespoons) to form a moderately stiff dough. Place in well-greased bowl, turning once to grease surface. Let both doughs rise till double, about 1 to 1¼ hours. Punch down. Cover the dough and let it rest on a lightly floured surface 10 minutes.

Roll out *half* the light dough and *half* the dark dough, each to a 12x8-inch rectangle. Place dark dough atop light dough; roll up tightly, beginning at short side. Repeat with remaining doughs. Place in 2 greased 8½x4½x 2½-inch loaf dishes. Cover and let rise till double, 45 to 60 minutes. Bake at 375° till done, 30 to 35 minutes. Makes 2 loaves.

Cream of Potato Soup Bread

> 2 packages active dry yeast
> 5½ to 6 cups sifted all-purpose
>   flour
> 1½ cups milk
> 2 tablespoons butter or margarine
> 2 tablespoons sugar
> 2 teaspoons salt
> 1 10½-ounce can condensed cream
>   of potato soup

Combine yeast and *2½ cups* of the flour. Heat together milk, butter, sugar, and salt just till warm, stirring occasionally to melt butter. Add to dry ingredients in mixer bowl; add potato soup. Beat at low speed of electric mixer for ½ minute, scraping sides of bowl. Beat 3 minutes at high speed. By hand, stir in enough of remaining flour to make a moderately stiff dough. Turn onto lightly floured surface. Knead till smooth, 5 to 8 minutes. Place in greased bowl, turning once. Cover; let rise till double, 50 to 60 minutes. Punch down. Cover; let rest for 10 minutes.

Divide dough in half; shape into two loaves. Place in two greased 8½x4½x2½-inch loaf dishes. Let rise till double, 25 to 30 minutes. Bake at 400° for 25 to 30 minutes. Makes 2.

Cheese Braid

Combine 1 package active dry yeast and 2 cups sifted all-purpose flour. Heat together 1½ cups milk, 2 tablespoons sugar, and 1½ teaspoons salt just till warm. Add to dry ingredients. Add 1 egg and 8 ounces process pimiento cheese, shredded (2 cups). Beat at low speed of electric mixer for ½ minute, scraping sides of bowl. Beat 3 minutes at high speed. By hand, stir in 2½ to 3 cups sifted all-purpose flour, enough to make a stiff dough. Turn onto lightly floured surface. Knead till smooth, 8 to 10 minutes. Place in greased bowl, turning once to grease surface. Cover; let rise till double, about 1½ hours. Punch down.

Divide dough in six pieces. Cover; let rest 10 minutes. Roll each piece into rope 15 inches long. On greased baking sheets, shape into 2 braids, using 3 ropes of dough for each loaf. Cover; let rise till almost double, 35 to 45 minutes. Bake at 375° for 15 to 20 minutes. Brush with melted butter. Makes 2 braids.

Sweet Banana Bread

Combine 2 packages active dry yeast and 2 cups sifted all-purpose flour. Heat together ¾ cup milk, ½ cup butter, ½ cup sugar, and 1 teaspoon salt just till warm, stirring occasionally to melt butter. Add to dry ingredients. Add 2 eggs and 2 ripe bananas, mashed (1 cup). Beat at low speed of electric mixer for ½ minute, scraping sides of bowl. Beat 3 minutes at high speed. By hand, stir in 3½ to 4 cups sifted all-purpose flour, enough to make a moderately stiff dough. Turn onto lightly floured surface. Knead till smooth, 5 to 8 minutes. Place in greased bowl, turning once. Cover; let rise till double, about 1 hour. Punch down. Let rest 10 minutes.

Divide dough in half. Shape into 2 round loaves; place on greased baking sheets. Make vertical cuts about ⅛ inch deep around each loaf at ¾-inch intervals.

Slightly beat 1 egg white with 1 teaspoon water. Brush over entire surface of loaves. Let rise again till double, 30 to 45 minutes. Bake at 400° for 30 minutes. Makes 2 loaves.

Refrigerated Herb Rolls

> 1 package active dry yeast
> 3¼ to 3½ cups sifted all-purpose
>   flour
> 2 teaspoons celery seed
> 1 teaspoon dried thyme leaves,
>   crushed
> 1¼ cups milk
> ¼ cup shortening
> ¼ cup sugar
> 1 egg

Combine yeast, *1½ cups* of the flour, celery seed, and thyme. Heat together milk, shortening, sugar, and 1 teaspoon salt just till warm. Add to dry mixture in mixing bowl; add egg. Beat at low speed of electric mixer for ½ minute, scraping sides of bowl constantly. Beat 3 minutes at high speed. By hand, stir in enough of the remaining flour to make a moderately soft dough. Place in greased bowl, turning once. Cover; chill at least 2 hours.

Shape into 18 cloverleaf rolls: Place three 1¼-inch balls in greased muffin pans. Brush with melted butter. Let rise till double, about 1 hour. Bake at 400° for 12 to 15 minutes.

Orange-Butter Coffee Cake

      2 packages active dry yeast
    ½ cup warm water
    ¼ cup granulated sugar
      2 eggs
    ½ cup dairy sour cream
      6 tablespoons butter or margarine,
        melted
      1 teaspoon salt
   3¾ cups sifted all-purpose flour
    ⅔ cup granulated sugar
      1 cup flaked coconut, toasted
      2 tablespoons shredded orange peel
      2 tablespoons butter or margarine,
        melted
      1 cup sifted confectioners' sugar
      3 to 4 teaspoons orange juice

Soften yeast in the warm water. In mixing bowl combine ¼ cup sugar, eggs, sour cream, 6 tablespoons melted butter, and salt. Stir in softened yeast. Gradually add enough of the flour to form a moderately stiff dough, beating well. Cover; let rise in warm place till double, about 45 minutes.

Combine ⅔ cup sugar, coconut, and orange peel. Knead dough a few strokes on well-floured surface. Roll *half* the dough to a 12x8-inch rectangle. Brush with *1 tablespoon* of the melted butter. Sprinkle with ½ *cup* of the coconut mixture. Roll up, starting with long side. Cut into twelve 1-inch slices. Place, cut side down, in greased 9x1½-inch round baking pan. Repeat shaping with remaining dough, butter, and another ½ cup coconut mixture. Let rise in warm place till light, 30 to 45 minutes. Sprinkle rolls with remaining coconut mixture. Bake at 350° till light golden brown, about 30 minutes. Remove from pans and cool right side up. Combine confectioners' sugar and orange juice. Drizzle over cooled coffee cakes. Makes 2 coffee cakes.

YELLOW PERCH—A freshwater fish of the perch family that is found mainly in the Great Lakes area. Commercially, it is a very important food fish with a sweet and firm flesh. (See also *Perch.*)

YERBA MATE *(yar' buh)*—Another name for the tealike beverage, maté, popular in South America. (See also *Maté.*)

YOGURT, YOGHURT, YOGHOURT *(yō' guhrt)*—A fermented, custardlike milk product having a tangy flavor. In the United States, yogurt is prepared from fresh, partially skimmed, cow's milk. In some countries, it is made from the milk of sheep, goats, or water buffalo.

The origin of yogurt dates back several thousand years to countries in the Middle East. The nomads of early times are thought to have carried yogurt in goatskins on their long journeys through the deserts. They discovered that this cultured, semisolid milk was safe to eat even after several days in the hot sun.

Although yogurt was a familiar food to people of other countries, it was not until the early twentieth century that the culture used in making yogurt was isolated. Dr. Illya Metchnikoff, who was Louis Pasteur's successor as director of the Pasteur Institute, was responsible for isolating the culture from Bulgarian yogurt. He named the culture *Bacillus bulgaricus.* For his work on yogurt, he received a Nobel Prize. Around 1940, commercial production of yogurt in America began.

The commercial method for preparing yogurt is to inoculate fresh, pasteurized, partially condensed milk with a culture that is taken from a previous batch of yogurt. The milk is usually partially skimmed, and nonfat dry milk solids are added. At this point, the milk is incubated for several hours at 105° to 115° until a curd forms. Flavorings are often added.

Yogurt is related to dairy sour cream because both are cultured dairy products. However, yogurt has fewer calories. One cup of plain yogurt made from skim milk has 125 to 150 calories, while one cup of dairy sour cream contains about 485 calories. The same amount of cream-style cottage cheese has 240 to 260 calories. The fruit-flavored yogurts contain more calories, averaging around 350 per cup, and they have sugar added.

Yogurt contains the same nutrients as does the milk from which it is made, making it a good source of calcium. In addition, it is easily digested by the body, and the lactic acid in yogurt aids in the digestion of other foods.

Since yogurt is a perishable dairy product, store it in the refrigerator as soon as possible after purchase.

Yogurt is gaining in popularity as a dairy product, especially since the introduction of the flavored varieties. People are discovering that plain and flavored yogurts are not only nutritious but they have a delicious flavor.

Plain yogurt can be substituted for dairy sour cream in many recipes, giving a more tangy flavor to the product. Like dairy sour cream, yogurt needs low cooking temperatures and a short heating period so that it doesn't separate. To prevent yogurt from separating during cooking, stabilize it with flour or cornstarch. Another tip to prevent yogurt from breaking down is to gently fold it in rather than vigorously stirring it.

Use yogurt as a sauce for vegetables, and in dips, spreads, salad dressings, casseroles and other main dishes, pies, and other desserts. Both plain and flavored yogurts are also delicious to eat as is without added ingredients.

Fruit Galaxy Salad

A low-calorie recipe—

  1 8-ounce can dietetic-pack
       pineapple tidbits
  1 tablespoon cornstarch
  2 tablespoons lemon juice
       Noncaloric liquid sweetener
       equal to ¼ cup sugar
  ½ cup plain yogurt
  1 cup sliced, fresh peaches
  1 cup diced, unpeeled apple
  ½ cup diced, fresh pear
  ½ cup sliced banana
  ½ cup halved, seedless green
       grapes

Drain pineapple tidbits, reserving ½ cup juice. In 1½-quart saucepan gradually stir pineapple juice into cornstarch. Stir in lemon juice and sweetener. Cook and stir over medium heat till thickened and bubbly; cool. Fold in yogurt, then pineapple, peaches, apple, pear, banana, and grapes. Chill salad for several hours before serving. Makes 8 servings.

Honeydew Stack-Up

Cut 1 honeydew melon into six ½-inch thick slices. Peel and remove seeds. Place each melon slice on lettuce-lined plate. Top with one 16-ounce can pitted, dark sweet cherries, drained and halved; and 6 peaches, sliced. Serve with *Blue Cheese Dressing:* Stir together ⅓ cup plain yogurt and 1 tablespoon sugar till blended. Then, stir in 2 tablespoons crumbled blue cheese. Makes 6 servings.

Yogurt Salad Dressing

  1 cup plain yogurt
  2 teaspoons milk
  1 teaspoon lemon juice
  ¼ teaspoon garlic salt
  ¼ teaspoon onion salt
       Dash dried rosemary leaves,
       crushed

Combine all ingredients; chill. Makes 1 cup.

Seasonal fresh fruits topped with yogurt and blue cheese dressing make Honeydew Stack-Up a great-tasting, low-calorie salad.

Cheese-Topped Pears

½ cup plain yogurt
¼ cup cream-style cottage cheese
2 tablespoons mayonnaise or
    salad dressing
1 tablespoon blue cheese
1 29-ounce can pear halves,
    drained and chilled

Blend together first 4 ingredients. To serve, spoon a little cheese mixture over center of each pear half. Makes ¾ cup dressing.

Strawberry Yogurt Medley

2 medium bananas, sliced
    Lemon juice
2 cups fresh strawberries, halved
2 medium oranges, peeled and
    sectioned
            • • •
½ cup strawberry yogurt
1 4-ounce package whipped cream
    cheese
2 tablespoons sugar

Dip bananas in lemon juice. Combine strawberries, orange sections, and bananas; chill. Stir yogurt into cream cheese; add sugar. Arrange fruit in compote; spoon on yogurt mixture. Or stir topping into fruit and serve in lettuce cups. Makes 4 to 6 servings.

Pineapple-Orange Yogurt Dip

1 8-ounce carton orange yogurt
    (1 cup)
⅓ cup chopped, fresh pineapple
2 tablespoons brown sugar
    Fresh pineapple cubes
    Whole fresh strawberries

Combine yogurt, chopped fresh pineapple, and brown sugar. Chill to blend flavors. To serve, dip pineapple cubes and strawberries in yogurt dip. Makes 1⅓ cups dip.

YOM KIPPUR *(yôm kip′ uhr)*—The Jewish high holy day, also called the Day of Atonement. It is a day of fasting (abstinence from food and drink), which follows the holidays of Rosh Hashanah.

The final meal eaten before sundown on the eve of Yom Kipper is a substantial one at which bland foods are served to prevent thirst during the following day of fast. (See also *Jewish Cookery*.)

YORKSHIRE PUDDING *(yôrk′ shēr, -shuhr)*—A favorite English, breadlike accompaniment traditionally served with roast beef. The pan of Yorkshire pudding was originally set under the meat roasting over an open fire. Baked in this way, it caught the meat drippings.

Contrary to its name, Yorkshire pudding is not a pudding as such. The batter is similar to a popover batter, and it is sometimes poured over the meat drippings in the roasting pan. Then, it's baked and cut into squares. However, Yorkshire pudding is easily baked and attractively served as individual portions, using custard cups. (See also *English Cookery*.)

Individual Yorkshire Puddings

2 eggs
1 cup milk
1 cup sifted all-purpose flour
1 tablespoon salad oil
    Beef drippings (about ¼ cup)

Place eggs in mixing bowl. Add milk, flour, and ½ teaspoon salt. Beat 1½ minutes with rotary or electric beater. Add salad oil and beat ½ minute longer. With some of the beef drippings, grease 6 to 8 custard cups. Place about 1 teaspoon additional drippings in each cup. Fill cups half full with batter. Bake at 475° for 15 minutes. Reduce heat to 350° and bake till browned and firm, about 25 minutes longer. Serve them piping hot with roast beef and gravy, or eat them as popovers. Makes 6 to 8 puddings.

Company-best dinner

Surround a Standing Rib Roast (see *Beef* for → recipe) with Individual Yorkshire Puddings, which are baked in custard cups.

Z

ZABAGLIONE *(zä' buhl yō' nē)*—An Italian dessert consisting of a foamy egg custard flavored with sugar and wine (usually Marsala). Constant beating over hot water enables the custard to become thick and frothy. The dessert is usually served in individual glasses, although it is sometimes used as a sauce. The French version of zabaglione is called sabayon.

Easy Zabaglione

This simplified version is uncooked—

> 1 3¾-ounce package vanilla
>   whipped dessert mix
> 1 egg
> ¼ cup sugar
> ⅓ cup dry sherry

In a small, deep bowl thoroughly blend vanilla whipped dessert mix and ½ cup water. Whip at highest speed of electric mixer for 1 minute. (Mixture will be quite thick.) Add ¾ cup water. Whip at high speed till mixture thickens, about 4 minutes; set the mixture aside.

Beat egg till thick and lemon-colored, 3 to 5 minutes. Gradually add sugar, beating till mixture is very thick. Blend egg mixture and wine into whipped dessert mix. Chill at least 1 hour. Before serving, stir till smooth. Serve over chilled fresh or canned fruit. Serves 8.

ZEST—1. The thin, bright-colored outer portion of orange, lemon, or lime peel. This part, rich in the flavor of the fruit oils, is used for grated peel. **2.** The oil extracted from this outer peel.

ZINFANDEL—1. A grape variety grown primarily in California. **2.** The name of a red wine made from these grapes.

This grape variety and wine hold an aura of mystery since it is not known where the grapes themselves or the name they were given originated. However, zinfandel grapes and wine are almost exclusively produced in California. The fruity, spicy, and zesty wine is of the claret type. (See also *Wines and Spirits.*)

ZITI *(zē' tē)*—A large, smooth, tubular macaroni with a diameter of one-fourth to one-half inch. (See also *Macaroni.*)

ZUCCHINI SQUASH—A summer squash variety of Italian origin. Other names for this squash include Italian marrow, Italian squash, baby marrow, and courgette. Zucchini have an almost straight, cylindrical shape that gradually enlarges toward the base. The rind is a deep green with pale yellow spots that almost group in stripes. Although zucchini can grow quite large, they are preferred for eating when about five to seven inches long.

Nutritional value: From a half-cup serving of cooked zucchini comes a wide assortment of valuable nutrients: a good amount of vitamin C; fair amounts of vitamin A and the B vitamin niacin; lesser levels of other vitamins and minerals; and approximately 15 calories.

How to select and store: Fresh zucchini are available in largest quantities during the summer. Choose squash that are heavy for their size, have glossy, deep green rinds, and are relatively small and straight. Large zucchini are less tender and flavorful than are the small ones.

At home, use zucchini squash as soon as possible. If zucchini must be held a few days before use, store them in the refrigerated vegetable keeper.

How to prepare: Zucchini is one of the most versatile squash varieties since it is tender enough to serve raw or cooked. Either way, the skin is left on. For added attractiveness, the rind may be scored lengthwise with fork tines.

Zucchini flavor and texture are preferred when cooked to the crisp-tender stage. Cook sliced or cubed zucchini in

Easy Zabaglione, a modernized variation of the Italian dessert, blankets a fruit cup. Another time, use it as a cake sauce.

boiling, salted water for 8 to 15 minutes. Or slice and fry it in butter for 5 minutes, covered, then about 5 additional minutes, uncovered. Bake zucchini half shells.

How to use: In the uncooked state, serve zucchini as a dipper for dips and dunks or as an ingredient in tossed salads. For a buffet, surround a mound of potato salad with sliced zucchini, tomato wedges, and asparagus spears.

Cooked zucchini is attractive when baked "on the half shell" or when sliced and dressed with a clear or creamy sauce. Because of its mild flavor, zucchini blends well with tomatoes, cheese, onion, eggs, and various seasonings such as garlic and herbs. It's fun and easy to prepare this squash because it has so many uses and cooks so quickly. (See also *Squash*.)

Zucchini Parmesan

    3 cups thinly sliced zucchini
      squash
    2 tablespoons butter or margarine
    ½ teaspoon salt
      Dash pepper
          • • •
    2 tablespoons grated Parmesan
      cheese

Cook zucchini, covered, with butter, salt, and pepper in skillet over low heat for 5 minutes. Uncover and cook, turning slices, for 5 minutes more. Sprinkle with cheese. Serves 4.

Zucchini Half-Shells

    6 small zucchini squash
          • • •
    ¼ cup butter or margarine
    1 tablespoon grated onion
    1 beef bouillon cube, crushed
    2 tablespoons water

Trim ends from zucchini; cut in half lengthwise. Melt butter in large skillet; add onion and bouillon cube. Add zucchini halves, cut side down, and cook till golden. Turn; add water. Cover and cook over low heat about 10 minutes more. Makes 5 or 6 servings.

Zucchini-Beef Bake

6 small zucchini squash
(1½ pounds)
1 pound ground beef
½ cup chopped onion
1½ cups soft bread crumbs
¼ teaspoon dried thyme leaves,
crushed
¼ cup butter or margarine
¼ cup all-purpose flour
2 cups milk
4 ounces sharp process American
cheese, shredded (1 cup)
1 tablespoon butter or margarine,
melted

Wash and remove ends from zucchini; cut in ½-inch slices. Cook in boiling, salted water till tender, about 5 minutes; drain. In skillet cook meat with onion till meat is brown; drain off excess fat. Stir in ½ *cup* bread crumbs, ¾ teaspoon salt, thyme, and ⅛ teaspoon pepper. Remove the mixture from heat.

In saucepan melt ¼ cup butter; blend in flour and ½ teaspoon salt. Add milk all at once. Cook and stir till mixture thickens. Add cheese; stir till melted. Stir in meat.

Place *half* of zucchini in 2-quart baking dish; pour *half* cheese mixture over. Repeat. Combine remaining crumbs with 1 tablespoon melted butter. Sprinkle atop casserole. Bake at 350° for 30 to 35 minutes. Makes 6 servings.

Each serving of Spinach-Stuffed Zucchini is contained within one vegetable "boat." Cheese and bacon glamorize the squash halves, while tomato wedges and endive garnish the platter.

Sausage-Zucchini Boats

4 medium zucchini squash
   (2 pounds)
¼ pound bulk pork sausage
¼ cup chopped onion
   • • •
½ cup grated Parmesan cheese
½ cup fine cracker crumbs
1 slightly beaten egg
¼ teaspoon salt
¼ teaspoon dried thyme leaves,
   crushed
   Dash garlic salt
   Dash pepper

Cook whole zucchini in boiling, salted water till barely tender, 7 to 10 minutes. Cut in half lengthwise; scoop squash from shells and mash. cook sausage and onion in skillet; drain off excess fat. Stir in mashed zucchini. Reserve *2 tablespoons* Parmesan cheese; mix remaining cheese with ingredients.

Spoon filling into zucchini shells; place shells in shallow baking dish. Sprinkle with reserved Parmesan cheese; dash with paprika, if desired. Bake at 350° till heated through, 25 to 30 minutes. Makes 4 servings.

Spinach-Stuffed Zucchini

3 zucchini squash (about 1 pound)
1 10-ounce package frozen chopped
   spinach, cooked and well
   drained (about 1 cup)
2 tablespoons all-purpose flour
½ cup milk
⅓ cup shredded natural Cheddar
   cheese
4 slices bacon, crisp-cooked,
   drained, and crumbled

Trim off ends of zucchini; cook whole in boiling water for 10 to 12 minutes. Drain thoroughly. Halve lengthwise and scoop out centers; chop centers. Add zucchini to spinach.

In saucepan blend flour and milk; add spinach mixture. Cook, stirring constantly, till thickened. Place zucchini halves in shallow baking dish; sprinkle cavities with salt. Spoon spinach mixture into zucchini shells. Top with cheese and bacon. Bake at 350° for 15 to 20 minutes. Makes 6 servings.

Cheddar-Squash Bake

A good way to use leftover zucchini—

6 cups thinly sliced, unpeeled
   zucchini squash
2 slightly beaten egg yolks
1 cup dairy sour cream
2 tablespoons all-purpose flour
2 stiffly beaten egg whites
1½ cups shredded Cheddar cheese
   • • •
6 slices bacon, crisp-cooked
   and drained
1 tablespoon butter or margarine,
   melted
¼ cup fine dry bread crumbs

Cook squash in boiling, salted water till crisp-tender; drain. Salt cooked squash. Combine egg yolks, dairy sour cream, and flour; fold in egg whites. Layer *half* the squash, egg mixture, and cheese in 11¾x7½x1¾-inch baking dish.

Crumble bacon; sprinkle over casserole. Repeat layers using remaining squash, egg mixture, and cheese. Mix melted butter and bread crumbs; sprinkle over top. Bake at 350° for 20 to 25 minutes. Makes 8 to 10 servings.

Frittata

4 slices bacon, diced
1 cup chopped zucchini squash
1 10-ounce package frozen chopped
   spinach, cooked and drained
¼ cup chopped onion
½ teaspoon salt
   Dash pepper
   Dash ground oregano
   • • •
6 eggs
2 tablespoons Parmesan cheese

Cook bacon; drain. Add zucchini, spinach, and onion. Stir well; cook for about 5 minutes. Season with salt, pepper, and oregano. Beat eggs till fluffy; add Parmesan cheese. Pour vegetable mixture into eggs; mix well.

Return entire mixture to frying pan; cover and cook over low heat till slightly browned on bottom, about 5 minutes. Place in a 350° oven for 10 minutes. Loosen omelet; slide onto warm platter. Makes 4 servings.

Spanish Zucchini

Uses popular ingredients of Spain—

1½ teaspoons salt
½ teaspoon chili powder
Dash pepper

• • •

4 pork chops, cut ½ inch thick
½ cup uncooked long-grain rice
1 29-ounce can tomatoes
½ cup chopped green pepper
½ cup chopped onion
½ cup chopped, pitted ripe olives
1 tablespoon sugar
2 cups thinly sliced, unpeeled
  zucchini squash

• • •

¼ cup grated Parmesan cheese

Mix salt, chili powder, and pepper. Trim fat from pork chops and heat trimmings in skillet until 2 tablespoons fat accumulate. Remove trimmings and brown the chops; season with *1 teaspoon* of the chili mixture. Drain off fat. Add rice, tomatoes, green pepper, onion, olives, and sugar. Border with zucchini; sprinkle all with remaining chili mixture.

Cover; cook, stirring occasionally, till pork is done, about 1 hour. Top with Parmesan cheese; cover skillet to melt cheese. Serves 4.

Spanish Zucchini, a meal-in-one dish, offers chili-spiced pork chops cooked with rice, zucchini, and assorted vegetables.

ZUBROVKA, ZUBROWKA (*zōō brōōf′ kä*) —A Polish vodka flavored with the bitter-tasting grass of the same name. The grass gives this liquor a light goldish green cast. A wisp of the dried grass is included in every bottle. (See also *Vodka.*)

ZUPPA INGLESE (*zōō′ puh in glā′ zā*) —A dessert made with cake, rum, and a filling. Translated, it means English soup, but in reality it's an Italian dessert. Like English Trifle, it consists of rum-soaked sponge cake layered with custard or whipped cream. Candied fruit often acts as a garnish for this dessert.

ZWIEBACK (*zwī′ bak,′ -bäk′*) —A specially formulated slice of slightly sweetened hard bread. The German word *zwei-bachen*, which gives the bread its name, means twice-baked.

The bread dough for zwieback is usually flavored lightly with lemon and cinnamon. The baked loaves are cooled, cut into slices, then oven-toasted at a low temperature until dried and golden brown.

Zwieback is an old-fashioned food for babies, given to them to exercise their gums when cutting teeth. Soaked in hot milk, it's good for convalescents.

Zwieback Meatballs

Combine 1 beaten egg, ⅓ cup milk, ½ cup crushed zwieback (4 to 5 slices), 1 tablespoon finely chopped onion, ½ teaspoon salt, ¼ teaspoon ground nutmeg, and dash pepper. Add 1 pound ground beef; mix well. Shape mixture into 20 meatballs. In skillet brown meatballs with 1 tablespoon hot shortening. Remove meatballs from skillet; discard the drippings.

Dissolve 1 beef bouillon cube in ¾ cup boiling water. Blend 2 tablespoons all-purpose flour with ¼ cup cold water. In skillet stir flour mixture into bouillon. Cook and stir till mixture is thickened and bubbly. Return the meatballs to skillet. Cover the mixture and simmer 20 minutes. Makes 4 or 5 servings.

ZWIEBEL—The German word for onions. The word is used in the names of some recipes containing onions.

INDEX

The index on the following pages has been designed to make it easy for you, the busy homemaker, to find the specific recipe you are searching for. Each recipe in the 18 volumes is listed not only by its title, but is also listed by its major category where appropriate, such as casserole, cookie, beverage, salad, dessert, or type of meat. Where necessary, the recipe is listed again by its major ingredient.

For example, Crisp Pecan Slices is listed under the first word in its title, *Crisp*. It's also listed under the nut, *Pecan*. If there were any other major ingredients listed in the title, it would be listed there too. This recipe is a cookie, so you'll find it in the general category *Cookie*. Because the recipes are cross-referred in this manner, you should be able to quickly and easily find just what you want.

To help you still further, some of the major categories, such as *Bread*, *Casserole*, and *Salad* are further divided into smaller groups for ease in finding a particular recipe quickly. As examples, you will find the *Bread* category divided into convenience, quick, and yeast; the

Casserole category divided into main dish and vegetable; and the *Salad* category divided into fruit, main dish, and vegetable.

There are also special categories for *Foreign Cookery* and *Regional Cookery*. You will find all kinds of favorites, from regional Jambalaya to a foreign favorite, Pfeffernuesse. In addition, listed under *Menus* are all the menu plans—breakfast, brunch, dinner, low calorie, lunch, supper, and other occasions—contained in the 18 volumes of the encyclopedia.

The index also contains all of the major articles presented in the encyclopedia. These are listed in all capital letters.

The numbers at the end of each listing will make the index easy for you to use. As an example, Beef Burgundy is listed on **3**·312. The **3** in heavy type indicates that the recipe is located in volume 3, and the 312 in light type designates the page number in that volume. When the reference listing reads **PEACH** . . . . . . **12**·1617-1626, this means that it is a major article and that you will find information on this particular subject from page 1617 through page 1626.

Reference to Charts and Tips

Recipe Index

A

APPLE . . . . **1**·79-96

Apple *continued*

C

CANDY . . . . **3**·375-386

CANNING . . . . **3**·388-400

Cantaloupe

Caper

Caramel

Caraway

Carrot

CASSEROLE . . . . **3**·423-430
Main Dish

Cereal

Charlotte Russe

Cheddar

CHEESE . . . . **4**·461-472

Cheese *continued*

Cheese *continued*

E

H

M

ORIENTAL COOKERY. 11·1543-1555

P

Peanut

Peanut Butter

Pecan

Peppermint

Peppy

Perch

Perfect

Pheasant

Pickle

POULTRY........... **13·**1781-1786
(See also *Chicken, Cornish Game Hen, Duck and Duckling, Goose, Turkey.*)

Pound Cake

Prune

Pudding

R

U

V

W

WINES AND SPIRITS . **18**·2465-2484

Acknowledgments

We are indebted to the following companies, agencies, and associations for the help they have given us in supplying or verifying the technical material in the Encyclopedia of Cooking.

Companies

Almadén Vineyards
American Molasses Company
G. Armanino & Son, Inc.
Asgro Seed Company
Ball Brothers Company
Best Foods
Del Monte Corporation
Encyclopaedia Britannica, Inc.
Foods from France, Inc.
Frito-Lay, Inc.
General Electric Company
General Foods Corporation
Heinz USA
Heublein, Inc.
Kellogg Company
Knox Gelatine, Inc.
Kraft Foods
McCormick & Co., Inc.
Morton International, Inc.
National Presto Industries, Inc.
Ocean Spray Cranberries, Inc.
Oscar Mayer & Co.
Paul Masson Vineyards
The Pillsbury Company
The Quaker Oats Company
Reynolds Metals Company
Sears, Roebuck and Co.
Standard Brands Incorporated
Sunkist Growers
Swift & Company
Taylor Instrument
The Taylor Wine Company
United Fruit Company
Universal Foods Corporation
Widmer's Wine Cellars, Inc.

Governmental Agencies

Iowa State Extension Service,
  Polk County
Minnesota State Extension Service,
  Beltrami County
United States Department of
  Agriculture; Agricultural Research
  Service, Consumer and Food
  Economics Research Division
United States Department of
  Agriculture; Consumer and
  Marketing Service, Information
  Division
United States Department of
  Agriculture; Consumer and
  Marketing Service, Poultry Division
United States Department of
  Commerce; National Oceanic and
  Atmospheric Administration,
  National Marine Fisheries Service
United States Department of
  Health, Education, and Welfare;
  Public Health Service, Food and
  Drug Administration
University of Kentucky, Extension
  Service, Lexington

Trade Associations

American Blue Cheese Association
American Dairy Association
American Honey Institute
American Lamb Council
American Meat Institute
The American Mushroom Institute
American Spice Trade
  Association
The Bourbon Institute
California Almond Growers
  Exchange
California Avocado Advisory Board
California Date Administrative
  Committee
California Raisin Advisory
  Board
California Olive Association
California Prune Advisory Board
Cereal Institute, Inc.
Chocolate Information Council
Diamond Walnut Growers, Inc.
Dried Fig Advisory Board
Dry Pea and Lentil
  Commissions
Durum Wheat Institute

Evaporated Milk Association
Florida Citrus Commission
Idaho Bean Commission
International Apple Institute
Licensed Beverage Industries, Inc.
National Association of Margarine
  Manufacturers
The National Broiler Council
National Canners Association
National Dairy Council
National Fisheries Institute
National Live Stock and
  Meat Board
The National Macaroni Institute
National Pork Producers
  Council
National Turkey Federation
Pan-American Coffee Bureau
The Popcorn Institute
Poultry and Egg National Board
Produce Packaging and Marketing
  Association, Inc.
Rice Council
The Roquefort Association, Inc.
Spanish Green Olive
  Commission
Stainless Steel News Bureau
Sugar Information, Inc.
Tea Council of the U.S.A. Inc.
United States Brewers Association
Washington State Apple
  Commission
Washington State Fruit Commission
Western Growers Association
Western Iceberg Lettuce, Inc.
Wheat Flour Institute
Wine Institute

We are also indebted to the following contributing editors for their assistance in researching and/or writing several of the articles.

Barbara MacDonald
Evelyn Miller
Agnes Murphy
Eleanor Noderer
Theodore Purdy
Rosalie Riglin